Money and Banking

Money and Banking

An Intermediate Market-Based Approach

William D. Gerdes

businessexpert
Press

Money and Banking: An Intermediate Market-Based Approach
Copyright © William D. Gerdes, 2014.

First published in 2014 by
Business Expert Press, LLC
222 East 46th Street, New York, NY 10017
www.businessexpertpress.com

ISBN-13: 978-1-60649-746-3 (paperback)
ISBN-13: 978-1-60649-747-0 (e-book)

Business Expert Press Economic collection

Collection ISSN: 2163-761X (print)
Collection ISSN: 2163-7628 (electronic)

Cover and interior design by Exeter Premedia Services Private Ltd.
Chennai, India

First edition: 2014

10 9 8 7 6 5 4 3 2 1

Printed in the United States of America.

Abstract

The premise of the author is that the study of money should commence at the most general level. Consequently, the book is anchored in the context of ***monetary systems*** (commodity, fiduciary, and fiat monies). The intent is to give the student of money a very broad perspective. It allows them to understand, for example, how the money we use today differs from money used in the past, or how our current money relates to money discovered by anthropologists in isolated subcultures.

Money is a market phenomenon. It originated as a spontaneous social institution, and its use is still inextricably tied to market exchange. Therefore, the analysis of money occurs in a ***market setting***. Use of monetary systems and a market setting as the underlying parameters ideally positions the reader to examine money in its various uses: as a medium of exchange, in credit markets, and as an instrument of monetary policy.

The material in the book is suited for ***upper-division college students*** and ***business professionals*** with an interest in money and banking systems.

The book is appropriate for use in traditional ***money and banking*** courses, but its potential use extends beyond that—to the undergraduate courses in ***monetary theory*** and as a sourcebook on money.

Keywords

fiat money, interest rates, inflation and the secular decline in the value of money, seigniorage, Austrian views on money and interest rates, monetary policy and its shortcomings.

To Linda

Contents

CHAPTER 1

Money and Monetary Systems

Money, Barter, and Exchange

Apart from the act of production, voluntary exchange is the major means available for individuals to improve their material living standards. When two individuals engage in an exchange, the motive of each is to improve his or her welfare. Because each individual gives up something of lesser value for something they perceive to have greater value, the exchange is mutually beneficial. Both parties gain as a consequence of the transaction.

There are two general forms of voluntary exchange: barter and those involving money. Barter is a direct exchange, where goods and services are exchanged for other goods and services. A requisite for a barter transaction is the existence of a double coincidence of wants. Individual A, for example, possesses wheat but would like to exchange some of that wheat for a baseball glove. That individual must find another (individual B) who has a baseball glove he is willing to exchange for some wheat. If there are two such individuals, and they agree on a rate of exchange (e.g., two bushels of wheat for one glove), an exchange occurs.

Exchange involving the use of money is called indirect exchange. Rather than a direct exchange of goods as in barter, goods are exchanged for an intermediate good (money), which is then exchanged for other goods and services. At first, this appears to be less efficient since it requires an extra transaction. If it were less efficient, however, individuals would prefer barter to the use of money. In practice, that is not the case. Nearly all transactions that we observe involve the use of money.

What is money, and why is it that monetary transactions are the dominant form of exchange? Money is any *generally* accepted medium of exchange. While monies in use today are generally associated with governments, they are by nature more behavioral than governmental. They are a behavioral phenomenon in the sense that money is whatever individuals opt to use as an exchange medium.

The concept of money is necessarily dynamic because what people do select for use as money varies by time and place. In virtually every culture, money in use today differs from that used in the past. Moreover, at any point in time, one can observe different forms of money used in different locations. Money used for purchases in an African village market is different from the money used to settle bond transactions in the world's major money centers. Both are different from that used in an isolated subculture in Papua New Guinea.

Economists introduce the concept of transaction costs to explain the dominance of monetary transactions over barter transactions. These costs are the resources that individuals must invest to participate in an exchange. They are of three principal types: (a) information costs, (b) transportation costs, and (c) storage costs.

Information is not a free good. If it were, quantities and offer prices of all goods and services would be known by everyone. Since a single individual does not possess all this information, resources frequently must be invested to acquire additional information prior to an exchange. In the barter example earlier, the individual with wheat must use resources to seek out an individual with a baseball glove. Once a generally accepted exchange medium is in use, it requires fewer resources to sell the wheat for money, and to use the money to purchase a baseball glove. With fewer resources expended, the transaction costs of exchange are reduced.

A second type of transaction cost is transportation costs. The parties involved in an exchange must transport the items to be exchanged. Most monies are relatively easy to transport, and one can do so at a relatively low cost. It is not very difficult, for example, to carry one's wallet or checkbook to the market. In a barter economy, by contrast, individuals must often transport commodities (such as wheat) to the market at a considerably higher cost. Thus, the use of money normally reduces transaction costs due to its relative ease of transport.

Finally, storage costs arise because of the necessity of storing items that are to be traded at a later date. Like other transaction costs, they normally cannot be avoided. In the case of barter, storage costs tend to be relatively high because of the greater number of commodities one must stock, and because some of them deteriorate while in storage. An example of the latter is grain spoilage that occurs during its holding period. In contrast to barter, money is generally less costly to store although there are storage costs here too. Today, they often assume the form of either service fees charged by banks or the erosion in the purchasing power of money due to inflation.

Because the use of money generally reduces the costs of engaging in voluntary exchange, the assumption is that its use greatly increases the number of exchanges that occur. Given that every voluntary exchange is wealth enhancing, the use of money contributes in a major way to improvements in our living standards.

Secondary Functions of Money

Money is defined in terms of its primary function: a medium of exchange. However, it serves other functions as well: as a store of value, unit of account, and standard of deferred payment. These are referred to as the secondary functions of money because they generally derive from its use as a medium of exchange.

The store of value function of money refers to its use as a vehicle for transferring purchasing power through time. It performs this function even when it is held for relatively short periods of time as an exchange medium. But, it also serves as a store of value when it is held for longer periods as a form of accumulated wealth.

Money also serves as a unit of account (or measure of value). In a monetary economy, the exchange value of all goods and services is quoted in terms of money, and comparative valuations are made by referring to monetary values of objects. If a watch sells for $100 and a tennis racquet for $200, we say that the tennis racquet is twice as valuable as the watch.

A final function of money is that it is customary to write loan contracts in terms of money. In this function, money is referred to as a standard of deferred payment. It is not necessary that money serve this function. It is possible, for example, to write a loan contract in which the proceeds of the loan (and subsequent repayment) are payable in corn, wheat, or any other commodity. It is unlikely, however, that both parties in a loan contract would find one of these commodities agreeable. As a consequence, virtually all credit contracts involve payment in money.

Properties of Money

Many different objects have served as money: cattle, seashells, beads, calico cloth, animal skins, tobacco, and precious metals. Despite the wide variety of forms of money, there are certain properties that all monies tend to possess. These properties share a common feature. Their presence often reduces the transaction costs associated with the use of money in exchange activities. The various forms of money tend to possess these properties in different degrees.

Four properties are discussed here. One is portability. Most objects selected for use as money can be readily transported to the market. Animal skins are more portable than animals, metal coins are more portable than animal skins, and paper money is more portable than metal coins. It is apparent that reducing transaction costs through greater portability was an important consideration in the evolution of money.

A second common property of money is divisibility. In the marketplace, items with a wide range of exchange values are traded. Money that is more divisible has greater value because it can be used in purchasing both relatively high and relatively low value goods. Cattle, when used as money, do not have this divisibility feature. Precious metals do, as do the more modern forms of money.

Third, most monies are durable. If money does not have this property, it will lose exchange value between the time it is accepted in exchange and the time when it is offered again in exchange. This probably explains why precious metals were a preferred form of commodity money. Even with the adoption of paper money, durability remains a matter of concern. Issuing governments want to know how soon such money will have to be replaced as a consequence of wear and tear.

Finally, most monies are objects that are relatively scarce. Transactions costs tend to be high when an object that is not scarce is used. That is because there is a high probability that such money will lose exchange value during the holding period. Precious metals, once again, are an example of money that is not easily augmentable. The production costs of doing so generally are substantial. Paper money, on the other hand, can be readily augmented in a short period of time. Our experiment with fiat money in the past century reveals that scarcity is one of the problems associated with using such money.

Types of Monetary Systems

There are three general types of monetary systems: commodity, fiduciary, and fiat.[1] Nearly all of our accumulated monetary experience is with commodity money. Fiduciary elements were introduced only in recent centuries, and it was not until the 20th century that nearly every society converted to the use of fiat money. From a broad historical perspective, then, the type of money used by nearly everyone today is a relatively new phenomenon.

Commodity money has one important identifying characteristic. Its value when used for monetary purposes tends toward equivalency with its value when used for nonmonetary purposes. Although a great number of different objects have been used as commodity money, precious metals were the most popular. Bronze, iron, and, more recently, silver and gold are metals that were most widely used for this purpose.

Fiduciary money differs from commodity money in two respects. First, its value when used as money exceeds its value when used for nonmonetary purposes. Second, it has a convertibility option. The convertibility option is typically a (paper) contract to pay a specified amount of commodity money on demand. Under the gold standard, for example, printed on a ten-dollar bill was the statement "Pay to the Bearer on Demand: Ten Dollars." When this note was presented to the issuer, the issuer was obliged to pay the bearer ten dollars in monetary gold.

Governments replaced fiduciary money arrangements with the fiat money standard that is currently in use. Fiat money has two distinctive features. Like fiduciary money, it has the property that its value when used as money exceeds its value when used for nonmonetary purposes.[2] The difference is the convertibility option. Fiduciary money is convertible (at issuing institutions) into commodity money on demand; fiat money is not.

This distinction is critical in understanding the origins of fiat money. Unlike commodity and fiduciary monies, fiat money was not a spontaneous market development. It did not result from the efforts of market participants to lower their transaction costs. Instead, it came about through the efforts of governments to gain greater control over money. Already active in the monetary process, 20th century governments invoked laws abrogating the convertibility option. Although this most recently happened in the 1930s, the history of fiduciary money standards is marked by earlier episodes where governments had suspended the convertibility option.

Governments found it particularly difficult to refrain from doing this during wartime. They were anxious to gain claims on more resources in order to prosecute the war effort. Although higher taxes always were an option, governments most often opted instead for printing more money. This choice places considerable stress on a fiduciary money system by significantly increasing the quantity of fiduciary money in use relative to commodity money. Ultimately, this jeopardizes the ability of issuers of fiduciary money to convert that money back into commodity money on demand. As a way around this problem, governments often passed laws suspending convertibility. Great Britain did this during the Napoleonic Wars as did the major adversaries during World War I.

The politics (and economics) of re-establishing fiduciary money arrangements after wars ended were both tedious and divisive. It took Great Britain nearly a decade to restore the gold standard after World War I. Shortly after she had done so, the major trading countries were caught in the midst of the Great Depression. Once again they suspended convertibility, but this time it was not a temporary expedient. Governments were too eager to wrest control of money from the private sector.

By now, however, individuals were quite accustomed to using paper money to effectuate exchanges. Under the fiduciary money standard, most individuals opted to make payment with paper money because of lower transaction costs. Thus, movement to the fiat money standard did not require a significant modification of their behavior. Nonetheless, consumers did have a preference for fiduciary money.[3] This meant that governments (such as that in the United States) found it necessary to impose laws making it illegal for individuals to hold commodity money in order to discourage further usage.[4]

Exhibit 1.1 summarizes the differences among the three monetary arrangements, which are: (a) whether money has the same value when used for monetary and nonmonetary purposes and (b) whether money is convertible into a specified amount of commodity money on demand (at financial institutions).

Exhibit 1.1 Characteristics of Different Monies

Type of money	Equivalent value in monetary and nonmonetary use	Greater value in monetary use	Convertibility option
Commodity	x		
Fiduciary		x	x
Fiat		x	

Inflation, Deflation, and the Value of Money

While one of the functions of money is the unit of account function, it is not fruitful to express the exchange value of money in terms of money. Doing so always yields the trivial value of one. The number of U.S. dollars that exchanges for one unit of U.S. money (one dollar) is precisely one. Likewise, the number of British pounds that exchanges for one unit of U.K. money (one pound) is also one.

As an alternative, money is viewed as generalized purchasing power, with its exchange value determined by how it exchanges against all other things. In this sense, the exchange value of money, or the purchasing power of money (PPM), is the reciprocal of the average price (P) of things other than money. (P is sometimes referred to as the price level.)

$$PPM = 1/P, \qquad\qquad (1.1)$$

where $P = (\overline{P_1, P_2, P_3, \ldots P_n})$

The reciprocal of P (the value of money) is subjectively determined by the users of money. Each price in P reflects how many units of money consumers are willing to exchange for one unit of that good. With each of those prices subjectively determined, the average of those prices is also determined subjectively. Thus, the value of money, in general, reflects the willingness of consumers to exchange money against goods and services more generally.

Because valuation is a subjective phenomenon, individuals can and do change their minds about the value of things. This is true for money too. Consequently, the value of money is subject to continuous variation.

Money loses value when consumers value money less in relation to goods and services. When they are willing to spend, on average, more units of money for goods and services, the price level rises. Such a situation when P is increasing (and the PPM is decreasing) is known as inflation.

Deflation occurs when consumers value money more relative to goods and services. Consumers are willing to exchange fewer units of money, on average, for goods and services. When this occurs, the average price of goods and services (P) falls and the PPM rises.

Monetary Systems and the Value of Money

Historical data indicate that fluctuations in the value of money are intimately related to the type of monetary system in use. That has certainly been true for the United States. Figure 1.1 shows the price level for the U.S. economy for the period from the Revolutionary War until 2012. The 153-year period from 1780 to 1933 was predominately one where commodity and fiduciary monies were employed. While the value of money changed more or less continuously as expected, the period was generally one of long-run price stability. Indicative of this stability, the average price of goods and services in 1933 was very close to what it was in 1780—only about 6% lower.

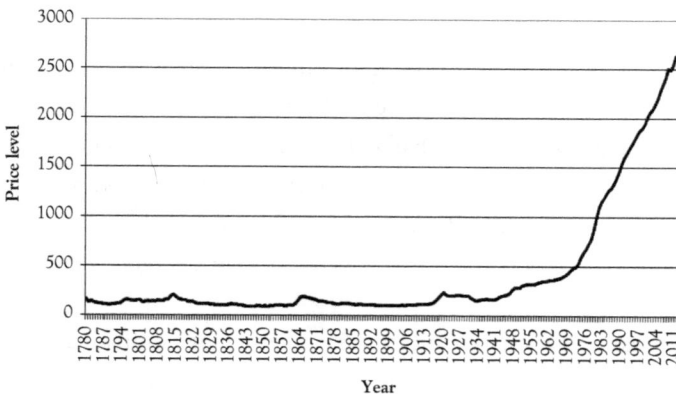

Figure 1.1 **The price level: United States, 1780–2012**

Sources: David and Solar (1977); U.S. Bureau of Labor Statistics (www.bls.gov/cpi).

This long-run stability in the value of money was not a historical accident. Economic analysis suggests that we are likely to experience greater long-run price stability if we use commodity or fiduciary money rather than fiat money. The reason is that market forces are present that tend to bring about long-run price stability with commodity or fiduciary money. There are no comparable market forces under a fiat money standard.

Consider the case of commodity money. An increase in the general price level is equivalent to a decline in the exchange value of money relative to goods and services. Because relative prices have moved in favor of goods and services, and against money, economic incentives exist for producers to employ more resources in the production of goods and services and fewer in the production of commodity money. The resulting reallocation of resources is shown in Figure 1.2. The decline in the production of money and the increase in the production of goods and services combine to dampen (and ultimately terminate) the upward pressure on the average price.

Those same market forces also render deflation self-limiting. With falling price levels, money gains exchange value relative to goods and services. Market incentives now encourage the allocation of more resources for the production of money and fewer for the production of goods and services (Figure 1.2).

In the case of gold-based money, for example, producers of gold now have an incentive to devote more resources to the discovery of new sources of that commodity. Those same producers may also invest additional resources to develop new technologies that improve mining and refining techniques in the gold mining industry. The long-term results of such activities are an increase in the production of gold, an increase in commodity money, and an eventual end to deflation.

The cogency of these arguments is unaffected with the introduction of fiduciary money. The major difference is that, in the short run, it is

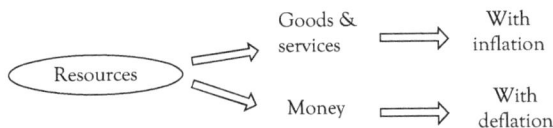

Figure 1.2 Changes in the value of money and resource reallocation

possible for governments (or banks) to adjust the quantity of fiduciary money and temporarily neutralize the effect of movements in relative prices on the production of commodity money. That is not possible, however, in the long-run.

With inflation, what limits the continued issue of fiduciary money is the convertibility option. The introduction of more and more fiduciary money to offset the declining production of commodity money results in a decline in the ratio of commodity money to fiduciary money. This cannot occur indefinitely because the stability of the financial system eventually is jeopardized. If enough users of fiduciary money become concerned that they will be unable to convert their fiduciary money into commodity money on demand, the potential for a bank run arises (i.e., a large-scale withdrawal of commodity money from banks). This threat discourages the introduction of additional fiduciary money and inflation ultimately subsides.[5]

There are no such automatic forces that make for long-run price stability under a fiat money standard. The U.S. experience with fiat money affirms this. Through an executive order, President Franklin D. Roosevelt forced the country off the gold standard in March 1933. Previously, market forces, manifested in the form of the convertibility option, constrained how much fiduciary money the U.S. government could print. Elimination of the convertibility option removed that constraint.

In Figure 1.1, it is easy to see when the change in monetary regimes occurred. The Government was now in a position to print any amount of fiat money it so chose. The preference of the U.S. government was to continuously augment the quantity of money; the consequence, secular inflation. Under the fiat money standard, the U.S. dollar lost approximately 94% of its purchasing power from 1933 to 2012.

The exodus from fiduciary money in the 1930s was international in scope. The motive for other countries was similar to that of the United States—to give government greater control over money. That objective was achieved, but what governments accomplished with their enhanced monetary powers has generally been unimpressive.

One major global outcome has been the adverse impact of governments on the flow of services provided by money. In many cases, those services were severely diminished. Discussed in Chapter 5, this reduced flow of services was a direct by-product of the sharp decline in the exchange value of fiat monies. In nearly all countries, the depreciation was much worse than the 94% experienced in the United States. For a global perspective on the declining value of fiat monies, refer to Table 5.2.

Measures of Money

There are several different measures of money. Two are discussed here: M1 and M2. The M1 measure, which is sometimes called the "narrow" measure, most closely conforms to the definition of money as a generally accepted exchange medium. Depicted in equation (1.2), it consists of currency in circulation outside banks (C), demand deposits other than those owned by the central government (DD), other checkable deposits (OCD), and traveler's checks (TCK). When demand deposits, other checkable deposits, and traveler's checks are aggregated, they are designated as total checkable deposits, or DD√.

$$M1 = C + DD + OCD + TCK$$
$$= C + DD\sqrt{} \qquad (1.2)$$

Currency is the total of all circulating coins and paper notes. In the past, it was often issued by private mints or private banks, but currency issue is now largely in the domain of governments. The U.S. Treasury issues all coins in the United States, while the Federal Reserve System issues paper notes. Demand deposits are checking balances at depository institutions that are legally payable on demand. Both currency and demand deposits are widely used in making exchanges.[6]

Since the Great Depression, U.S. banks have not been permitted to pay interest on demand deposits. In the post-World War II period, this placed banking institutions at a competitive disadvantage in the financial marketplace. They responded (in the 1970s) by issuing a new type of deposit—interest-bearing savings deposits that allowed individuals to access funds in these accounts by writing a check. Examples were share drafts and negotiable order of withdrawal (NOW) accounts. These interest-bearing checking accounts were an enormous market success. Beginning in 1980, they were included in the M1 measure of money as other checkable deposits. They are so classified because, from a legal standpoint, they are not demand deposits.

A second measure of money is M2. It consists of all of the instruments in M1 plus additional financial instruments. Some of these instruments have check-writing privileges (certain money market deposit accounts and money market mutual fund shares). Other financial instruments in M2 are closely substitutable for checking deposits. Such money substitutes can be converted into deposit money with very low transaction costs. Included on these grounds are small-denomination time deposits, saving deposits (without check-writing privileges), overnight repurchase agreements, and certain overnight Eurodollar balances.

$$M2 = M1 + TD + SD + MMDA + MMMF + Other \qquad (1.3)$$
where TD is small time deposits,
SD is saving deposits,
MMDA is money market deposit accounts, and
MMMF is money market mutual fund shares.

While M1 more closely conforms to the definition of money, for a number of reasons the M2 measure is often utilized in economic studies.

CHAPTER 2

Money and Income

Fisher's Equation of Exchange

The equation of exchange was the mechanism employed by Irving Fisher to analyze the relationship between money and economic activity.[1] The basis for the equation was the proposition that there are two sides to every transaction: a buyer and a seller. Aggregating across all transactions, the total value of all things bought (B) is exactly equal to the total value of all things sold (S).

$$B \equiv S \qquad (2.1)$$

The right-hand side of the relationship is the goods side. The total value of all things sold (S) is equal to the sum of the price times the quantity for each item sold. Fisher wrote this as PT, where P is the average price and T is the total number of transactions. PT, then, is substituted for S on the right-hand side of equation 2.1.

The left-hand side is the money side. In a strictly monetary economy, all things are sold for money (M). However, it is not possible to substitute M for B on the left-hand side of equation 2.1 because it is very unlikely that each unit of money was used, on average, exactly one time in financing all exchanges (PT).

What relates money to spending is the velocity of circulation of money. Velocity (V_T), or transactions velocity, is the average number of times each unit of money is used in financing PT. It is now possible to represent total expenditures for goods and services as MV_T, and this term is substituted for B in equation 2.1. The result is Fisher's version of the equation of exchange.

$$MV_T = PT \qquad (2.2)$$

One problem with this version of the equation of exchange is that it is not operational. Fisher advanced the equation prior to the development of our system of national income accounts. Subsequent to the development of these accounts, Fisher's equation was modified to a form that was operational.

$$MV = Py \qquad (2.3)$$

where M is the money supply,

V is income velocity of money,

P is the average price of all final goods services sold, and

y is the number of final goods and services sold.

Modern governments measure both the money supply (M) and nominal gross domestic product (GDP). But, the right-hand side of 2.3 is nominal GDP. With measures for both M and Py, it is possible to calculate velocity (V). Consequently, this modified version of the equation of exchange is fully operational and, for that reason, generally is preferred to Fisher's original statement of the equation of exchange.

Before proceeding, this modified version of the equation of exchange (which is subsequently employed) is compared to Fisher's version. Py, or nominal GDP, is a measure of all final goods and services currently produced. Fisher's PT is the total value of all goods and services currently exchanged. Because many goods and services currently exchanged are not currently produced, Py is a proper subset of PT, that is, every good or service currently produced is contained in PT. Many things currently exchanged (and in PT), however, were produced in the past. Hence, they are not included in GDP. One such example is the sale of a used automobile.

With the same money supply (M), and with Py different from PT, the velocity terms in equations 2.2 and 2.3 are not the same. For that reason, they are represented by different symbols. Fisher's V_T is the number of times (on average) money is used in all exchanges. V, on the other hand, is the average number of times each unit of money is used in the financing of GDP expenditures. Because Py is smaller than PT, V is smaller than V_T.

Fisher's equation of exchange was criticized on the grounds that it was a tautology. Fisher's response was that just because a relationship is tautological does not mean it is without value. The equation of exchange is a case in point. Even though it is a tautology, it is a very useful device for analyzing factors responsible for changes in the purchasing power of money.

Based on the equation of exchange, all changes in the purchasing power of money are the result of changes in M, V, y, or in some combination of the three. The reason is that if P (and the purchasing power of money, 1/P) changes, something else in the equation of exchange must have changed as well. Otherwise, MV ≠ Py.

Increases in M bring about increases in P. Thus, they reduce the purchasing power of money (1/P). Increases in P can also result from a more frequent use of money. Hence, like M, V and the purchasing power of money are indirectly related. Increases in production (y), however, have the opposite effect. A greater production of goods and services, with the same amount of money, leads to lower prices for goods and services. That is the same thing as an increase in the exchange value of money.

To summarize, M and V are indirectly related to the purchasing power of money, while y is directly related. These relationships are shown in equation 2.4, which shows 1/P as derived from the equation of exchange.

$$1/P = y/MV \qquad\qquad (2.4)$$

Velocity and the Demand for Money

Cambridge University economists in England developed the theory of money in a manner that did not involve the equation of exchange. A.C. Pigou, for example, began his analysis by treating money like any other good. From his perspective, there is a market for money, and his approach was to analyze the supply and demand for money within that context. He was able to derive several money-spending relationships that were similar to those of Fisher.[2]

No detailed analysis of differences in the two approaches is undertaken here.[3] However, it is important to note the relationship between the demand for money and Fisher's velocity of circulation of money. The two are inversely related to one another. When individuals increase their demand for money balances, they tend to hold money for a longer period of time, and the velocity of circulation of money falls. Likewise, reductions in the demand for money tend to increase velocity. Individuals are spending money more frequently.

Derivation of the inverse relationship is shown in equations 2.5– 2.7. Note that velocity is a relative measure of the demand for money. It reveals how much money individuals collectively demand in relationship to GDP. Moreover, the relationship is in inverse form.

$$V = (Py)/M \qquad (2.5)$$

$$V^{-1} = 1/V = M/(Py) \qquad (2.6)$$

In monetary equilibrium, the quantity of money supplied (M) is equal to the nominal quantity of money demanded (M^d). Hence, M^d can be substituted for M in equation 2.6.

A second adjustment in 2.6 is also appropriate. If rational economic agents think in real terms, they typically demand money balances expressed in terms of goods and services. Consequently, the numerator and denominator on the right-hand side of equation 2.6 are both divided by the average price (P). The resulting relationship between velocity and the demand for *real* money balances (M^d/P) is stated in equation 2.7.

$$1/V = (M^d/P)/y \qquad (2.7)$$

When individuals collectively demand more real money balances in relationship to real GDP (y), velocity falls. Alternatively, relative reductions in real money demand result in an increase in the velocity of circulation of money.

When V is viewed as a proxy for money demand, a somewhat different interpretation of Fisher's equation of exchange (equation 2.3) is also implied. Money supply (M) and money demand (in inverse form V) interact to determine the level of nominal GDP. Either an increase in the money supply or a decrease in money demand causes money GDP to increase. A reduction in the money supply or a rise in money demand, bring about the opposite: a decrease in money GDP.

Money and the Economy

The equation of exchange is also useful in analyzing the relationship between money and the economy. If the money supply changes, the off-setting entry in the equation of exchange must be either V, P, or y (or some combination of the three). Those three possibilities are shown in Exhibit 2.1.

The Liquidity Trap

If increases in the money supply are absorbed in the form of a reduction in velocity, we are experiencing what John Maynard Keynes described as absolute liquidity preference. In this case, monetary policy has no effect on aggregate spending because individuals hold rather than spend any increase in the quantity of money. Keynes considered this case a theoretical curiosity: "Whilst this limiting case might become practically important in the future, I know of no example of it hitherto."[4]

While Keynes may have discounted its importance, that was not the case for his disciples (Keynesians). Rejecting Keynes' reticence, they renamed the phenomenon the liquidity trap and raised it to the level of a general case. The liquidity trap is something that routinely occurs during business cycle downturns. One of the more dramatic episodes, according to the Keynesians, was the Great Depression. During that cataclysmic decline, velocity decreases thwarted efforts by the Federal Reserve to end the depression through increases in the money supply.

When Keynesian economics attracted more followers in the 1950s and 1960s, the concept of the liquidity trap gained credibility. This had enormous policy implications. For, if monetary policy is unreliable,

		M	V $=$	P	y
A.	Liquidity trap	↑	↓		
B.	Money and real GDP	↑↓			↑↓
C.	Quantity theory of money	↑↓		↑↓	

Exhibit 2.1 Absorption of Money Changes Within the Equation of Exchange

its policy role is necessarily a secondary one. The ensuing relegation of monetary policy to the background made possible the major acceleration of money growth and the Great Inflation that plagued the U.S. economy in the late 1960s and the 1970s.

The discovery that activist economic policies lead to more inflation, and not higher living standards, placed followers of Keynes on the defensive. As Keynesian economics lost credibility, so too, did the concept of the liquidity trap. Significant in its demise were research findings published by Milton Friedman and Anna Schwartz in *A Monetary History of the United States*.[5]

An important component of their study was the construction of a money supply series for the United States back to 1860. This data led Friedman and Schwartz to reject the Keynesian interpretation of the Great Depression. The U.S. economy was not caught in a liquidity trap in the 1930s. In contrast to Keynesian assertions, it was not a situation where individuals were holding rather than spending Fed-induced increases in the money supply. The data revealed, instead, an unprecedented decline in the stock of money, which fell by 35% from 1929–1933. With a lack of empirical support for the existence of a liquidity trap, the concept was unceremoniously relegated to the position originally assigned to it by Keynes.

Money and Real GDP

If changes in money are not absorbed by changes in velocity, they affect spending. Through their impact the right-hand side of the equation of exchange, they bring about changes in the level of nominal GDP. Such changes in nominal GDP can, in turn, be further decomposed into changes in the average price (P), real GDP (y), or both.

Economists such as Irving Fisher, R.G. Hawtrey, and more recently, Milton Friedman argue that money affects spending differently in the short-run than in the long-run. In the short-run, changes in money primarily affect real magnitudes such as the level of production (y) and the employment of resources. Moreover, changes in M are considered the principal cause of business cycle fluctuations. These economists have what is called a monetary theory of the trade cycle. With fiat money controlled by central banks, it is governments that are the primary source of economic instability. It follows that the best prospect for taming the business cycle is for governments to provide greater monetary stability.

The long-run impact of changes in money is primarily on prices. This money-price nexus is exhibited historically by numerous cases of government debasement of money. One of the earliest episodes involved the Roman emperor, Nero, but the tradition is a robust one. It transcends different types of money and different forms of government. This long-run relationship between money and prices is formally known as the quantity theory of money.

The Quantity Theory of Money

The quantity theory of money is a misnomer. It is not a theory of money. Rather, it is a theory about what determines the long-run purchasing power of money. Fisher employed his equation of exchange as a mechanism to explain the quantity theory. It deserves mention that the equation of exchange alone is a tautology and not a theory. Hence, it is not sufficient to state that M and P are directly related to one another in the equation of exchange, *ceteris paribus*. That too, is a tautology.

To develop his version of the quantity theory of money, Fisher augmented the equation of exchange with two additional assumptions. First, he argued that, in the long-run, changes in the money supply do not affect the velocity of circulation of money. Other factors, however, do. He cited urbanization, changes in commercial customs (such as the use of credit), and changes in technology (e.g., improved transport) as causing velocity to change in the long-run. Hence, velocity was not a constant. It just wasn't affected by the money supply.

Second, in the long-run, changes in the money supply do not affect the level of production (y). If they did, we would have a guaranteed remedy for world poverty. Simply send printing presses to poor countries, and let them print massive quantities of fiat money. In fact, many of them have already tried this, but to no avail. The reason why this does not work is obvious. Printing additional fiat money does not increase wealth. By discouraging production, in many cases, it does just the opposite.

The observation that money does not affect production in the long-run does not imply that production is a constant. Long-run production obviously does change. According to Fisher, factors responsible for long-run increases in production are increased availability of resources and improvements in technology.[6]

Fisher's two assumptions are summarized in equations 2.8 and 2.9. Changes in the quantity of money (dM) have no long-run effect on either the velocity of money or the quantity of real GDP. The change in velocity (dV) and the change in real GDP (dy) with respect to a change in money are both equal to zero.

$$dV/dM = 0 \qquad\qquad (2.8)$$

$$dy/dM = 0 \qquad\qquad (2.9)$$

If money does not affect either V or y, it must affect P. That gives rise to Fisher's version of the quantity theory of money. Simply stated, in the long-run, a given change in the money supply occasions a direct and equi-proportionate change in the average price (relative to what it otherwise would have been).

Two things deserve mention here. First, while Fisher's quantity theory of money is a tautology as a theoretical exercise, it is not so empirically. It is possible for long-run changes in money to be reflected in something other than the average price. They could potentially be absorbed by velocity changes or changes in production.

Second, Fisher's theory does not state that long-run movements in M and P are equal to one another. The long-run movement in P is a resultant of the combined effects of changes in M, V, and y. While all three do have an influence, they are not all equally important. Fisher emphasized the relative importance of changes in money, which is a trademark of those in the quantity theory tradition.

A Dynamic Version of the Equation of Exchange

Hitherto, the analysis of money and the economy employed Fisher's equation of exchange expressed in terms of levels. The dynamic version of the equation of exchange expresses that same relationship in terms of growth rates.

$$dM/M + dV/V = dP/P + dy/y \qquad (2.10)$$

The following didactic exercises attempt to mimic historical episodes through the employment of this dynamic version of the equation of exchange.

Secular Deflation

The United States experienced secular deflation in the last one-third of the 19th century. This was a period of great innovations and rapid industrialization, and the U.S. growth rate for production was high by historical standards. The country was on the gold standard, and there were no new major discoveries of gold from mid-century until the late 1890s. As a consequence, production growth exceeded the growth rate for money. The result was a secular increase in the purchasing power of money.

Secular deflation of this type is portrayed as Case I in Exhibit 2.2. Real GDP is growing 4% per year, while the money supply is unchanged ($dM/M = 0$). Assuming no secular trend in velocity, the average price falls at the annual rate of 4%.

Case I has an important implication. It demonstrates that inflation is not a necessary condition for economic growth. To the contrary, by increasing the availability of goods and services, economic growth is actually *deflationary*. This deserves mention because the myth that inflation is necessary for economic growth was popular among development economists in the last half of the 20th century. Some contemporary economists and members of the popular media often expound a similar view.

	dM/M	+	dV/V	=	dP/P	+	dy/y
Case I	0		0		–4		4
Case II	4		0		0		4
Case III	8		0		4		4
Case IV	1,500		500		2,000		0

Exhibit 2.2 Dynamic Version of the Equation of Exchange

Alarmed when the U.S. inflation rate falls below 2%, they agonize about the potential dire consequences of deflation. The 19th century U.S. experience provides a good historical counterexample for those harboring such thoughts.

Secular Price Stability

For a country to experience secular price stability, money growth should approximate the long-run growth of production. That occurs in Case II, Exhibit 2.2. Both money growth and production growth are 4% per annum. Assuming no secular growth in velocity, the result is secular price stability.

Long-run price stability of this type does not imply that prices are stable every year. In some years, an economy might experience inflation; in others, deflation. For the entire period, however, the average price is stable. This was the U.S. experience with commodity and fiduciary monies. In 1933, the average price was approximately the same as it was in the early 1780s. (See Chapter 1, page 8, for a graph of the average price during this period.) Market forces, under these monetary standards, tend to bring about money growth rates that conform to the growth rate of production. That adjustment process was discussed on pp. 9–10.

The Quantity Theory of Money

In the dynamic version of the quantity theory of money, a given change in the growth rate of money (dM/M) occasions a direct and equi-proportionate change in the growth rate of the average price (dP/P) relative to what it otherwise would have been.

This dynamic version is illustrated by an economy that moves from Case II to Case III in Exhibit 2.2. The annual growth rate for money increases by 4%—from 4% percent in Case II to 8% in Case III. The ensuing rate of change in prices also increases by 4%, from 0% to 4% per year. While the quantity theory implies that the increase in the growth rate of the average price is equal the increase in the growth rate of money, note that it does not imply that the growth rates of money and the average price are the same. They are not in Case III.

As articulated by many in the late 19th century, inflation occurs when there is "too much money chasing too few goods." Money is growing more rapidly than is production (Case III). In that sense, Case III reflects the secular inflation in the United States following the imposition of fiat money in 1933. It is the result of too much money chasing too few goods.

Hyperinflation

Hyperinflation occurs when prices increase extremely rapidly. There is no threshold inflation rate where hyperinflation commences. Nevertheless, hyperinflation is generally not difficult to identify. It occurs exclusively under fiat money regimes, and can last for more than one year. However, it is not a long-run phenomenon. The process typically comes to an end when the government responsible for the hyperinflation announces that it is undertaking monetary reform. The reform usually assumes the form of a new fiat money. It is physically different from the previous fiat money, and often has a new name, for example, the real as opposed to the peso. A rate of exchange of the old for the new currency is announced (x-"kazillion" units of the old for one unit of the new). There were numerous such episodes under government stewardship of money following the departure from fiduciary money. A recent case was Zimbabwe.

Case IV, Exhibit 2.2, is a numeric example of what happens during hyperinflations. The central bank increases the money supply at the rate of 1,500% a year. With the money side of the equation of exchange increasing at this rate, great stress is transferred to the right-hand side of that equation. That stress is dissipated in the form of massive increases in prices.

This stress on the goods side (or right-hand side) of the equation of exchange is exacerbated by the behavioral response of owners of money balances. With hyperinflation, transactions costs in the form of storage costs for money increase dramatically. Simultaneously, large changes in relative prices are occurring, and everyone becomes an inadvertent speculator. The kind of portfolio adjustments individuals make in this environment matters a great deal. One type of portfolio adjustment, however, is not speculative. The purchase of almost any type of good is preferred to the ownership of money, and virtually all individuals soon learn to minimize their holding period for money balances. The result is a massive increase in the velocity of circulation of money. In Case III, the increase is 500% per year.

Reflecting pressures from both M and V, the annual inflation rate is now 2,000%. Although not portrayed in this example, the disruptive influence of this degree of monetary instability often leads to a significant decline in production (y). While very small when compared to the influences of M and V, this fall in production further erodes the purchasing power of money.

With M, V, and y all exerting upward pressure on P, the real money supply (or M/P) actually falls during hyperinflations. For some who focus on the real money supply, this can lead to the perverse interpretation that the economy is experiencing "tight money."

CHAPTER 3

Interest Rates and Financial Markets

Financial Markets

Financial instruments are traded in financial markets. The instruments are of two types. Equity instruments represent ownership in businesses, and are most often traded on organized stock exchanges. Debt instruments, or bonds, represent the borrowing of one economic agent from another. Organized exchanges where these instruments are traded are called bond markets.

Financial markets are critical for economic growth. The reason is that financial markets facilitate capital formation. Capital formation is important because the use of capital goods generally enhances human productivity. Hence, the availability and widespread use of capital goods is one of the prominent characteristics of relatively affluent countries. Relatively poor countries are characterized by the opposite—the limited use of capital goods and heavy reliance on human labor to carry out production. It is not surprising then that countries that discourage the development of financial markets generally languish. Those countries that encourage their development most often prosper.

Classification of Participants in Financial Markets

Saving, or the abstinence from consumption, is a requisite for capital formation. The act of saving releases resources for the production of capital goods or real investment. The production possibilities curve in Figure 3.1 shows this trade-off between consumption and investment. Each point on the curve is an ordered pair that represents an output combination that it is possible to produce. Constraints in effect include a given stock of resources and a given state of technology.

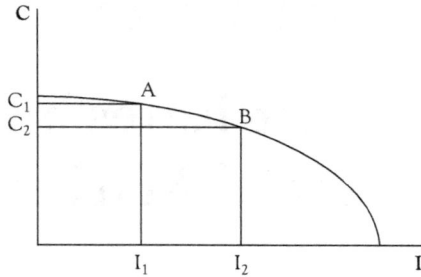

Figure 3.1 Production possibility curve.

Movement along the curve from point A to point B, for example, requires additional saving. More saving results in increased investment, and the production of capital goods increases from I_1 to I_2. This additional capital formation is made possible by abstinence from consumption, which falls from C_1 to C_2.

Flow of funds accounts, which provide a record of a country's financial flows, include an accounting identity that relates saving and investment. In the aggregate, total saving (S) is precisely equal to total investment (I).

$$S \equiv I \qquad\qquad (3.1)$$

Saving and capital formation can take place in an economy without financial markets. However, all capital formation must be internally financed. That is, the economic unit purchasing the capital goods must also provide the saving to finance that purchase.[1] In such an economy, aggregate identity 3.1 also holds for each individual economic unit.

The introduction of financial markets greatly increases the potential for capital formation. Now it is possible for the saving of one individual economic unit to finance the capital goods purchase of another economic unit. Because those wishing to purchase a capital good are no longer required to provide the requisite saving, the potential for capital formation is greatly enhanced. By facilitating capital formation, financial markets contribute in a significant way to the economic welfare of a society.

In an economy with financial markets, identity 3.1 still holds in the aggregate. However, it no longer must hold for individual economic units. Moreover, the relationship between saving and investment for the individual economic unit now serves as the criterion for classifying their participation in financial markets. Economic units whose saving exceeds their investment are called savings-surplus units (SSU). Those with investment greater than their saving are classified as savings-deficit units (SDU). Knife's-edge cases where saving is exactly equal to investment are neither savings-surplus nor savings-deficit units.[2]

Savings-Surplus Units

Savings-surplus units are net suppliers of funds to financial markets. The word net is critical because most economic units participate on both sides of financial markets. That is, they both demand and supply funds. A household, for example, may issue a mortgage to purchase a home and, during the same period of time, add to its demand or saving deposit balances at a commercial bank. Savings-surplus units are net suppliers because they supply more funds than they demand.

Each individual economic unit disposes of its income (Y) in the form of consumption expenditures (C), purchases of capital goods (I), or in the net accumulation of financial assets (Δ FA). If Δ FA > 0, the unit is purchasing more financial instruments (stocks and bonds) than it is issuing. The opposite is true when Δ FA < 0. This disposition of income for the economic unit is formally stated in 3.2.

$$Y = C + I + \Delta \text{ FA} \tag{3.2}$$

$$Y - C = S = I + \Delta \text{ FA} \tag{3.3}$$

Saving for an economic unit is the abstinence from consumption, or Y − C. As is apparent in equation 3.3, saving can assume two different forms. Real saving occurs in the form of capital goods purchases. In a world with no financial markets, this is the only form of saving. (With no stocks and bonds, Δ FA = 0 for every economic unit.) Financial saving, by contrast, occurs through the purchase of financial instruments.

As a net supplier of funds to financial markets, Δ FA > 0 for a savings-surplus unit. The unit shows a net accumulation of financial assets, as shown in equation 3.4. With income for the unit exceeding its expenditure on both consumer and capital goods, what is left over assumes the form of a net accumulation of financial assets.

$$Y - C - I = \Delta \, FA > 0 \tag{3.4}$$

$$Y - C = S > I \tag{3.5}$$

Equation 3.5 is the result when one transposes investment (I) to the right-hand side of the inequality in equation 3.4. This is a more common way of expressing the position of the savings-surplus unit. Savings of the unit exceeds investment for the unit.

Savings-Deficit Units

Savings-deficit units are net demanders of funds in financial markets. Their income is less than expenditures for consumer and capital goods. The position of this unit is presented symbolically in equation 3.6. In order to spend more than their income, these units become net issuers of financial instruments. In doing so, they demand funds in the financial marketplace.

Again, the more common way to describe the position of a savings-deficit unit is equation 3.7. Saving for the unit is less its purchase of capital goods (I).

$$Y - C - I = \Delta \, FA < 0 \tag{3.6}$$

$$Y - C = S < I \tag{3.7}$$

While an individual economic agent may be either a savings-surplus or savings-deficit unit, it is not possible for that to happen in the aggregate. The reason is that whenever someone issues a financial instrument, someone else purchases that instrument. Aggregation across all units produces a wash. That is, the net change in financial assets for all economic units (viewed collectively) is zero, i.e., $\Delta FA = 0$. If that is the case, then all aggregate saving is in the form of real saving ($S \equiv I$). These aggregate relationships are shown in equations 3.8 and 3.9.

Summing across all i consumers, income less the purchase of consumer goods and less the purchase of capital goods must sum to zero.

$$\sum_i (Y - C - I)_i \equiv 0 \quad i = (1,2,3,4,\ldots,n) \tag{3.8}$$

Partitioning that relationship yields the equality between aggregate saving and aggregate investment.

$$\sum_i (Y - C)_i \equiv \sum_i S_i \equiv \sum_i I_i \quad i = (1,2,3,4,\ldots,n) \tag{3.9}$$

Financial Flows

Net financial flows through markets are from SSU to SDU. The term net is significant because nearly all economic units participate on both sides of the financial marketplace. Households are the major savings-surplus units. Businesses and governments are the primary savings-deficit units. In a very general sense, then, financial flows are from the household sector to the business and government sectors of the economy.

These financial flows are depicted in Figure 3.2. The flows are referred to as direct finance if the flow from savings-surplus units to savings-deficit units does not involve financial intermediation. Without intermedia-

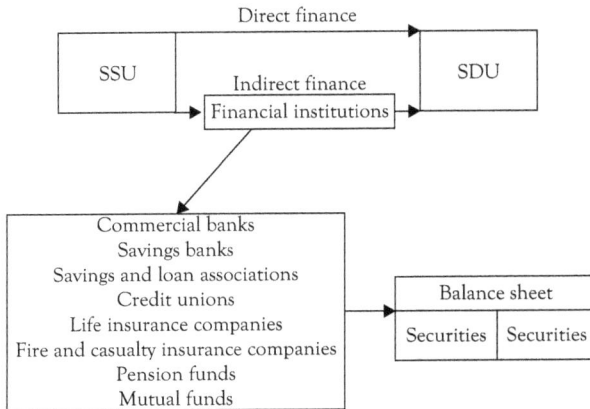

Figure 3.2 Financial flows

tion, the savings-surplus units actually purchase the securities issued by savings-deficit units. Such exchanges do not preclude the brokerage function. That is, a broker may bring these savings-surplus and savings-deficit units together.

Direct finance occurs, for example, when a household or a business purchases a U.S. Treasury-bill at the weekly T-bill auction. In this case, the U.S. government is a savings-deficit unit. It is issuing Treasury-bills to finance its deficit spending.

Households and businesses purchasing T-bills are savings-surplus units (so long as they are net suppliers of funds to financial markets). They are purchasing the new government debt. Because the weekly auctions of Treasury bills occur at Federal Reserve Banks, these Reserve Banks are performing a brokerage function.

A second example involves household purchases of bonds newly issued by a utility company. It is direct finance because these households are directly purchasing securities issued by a savings-deficit unit (the utility company). Again, households making such purchases are classified as savings-surplus units if they are net suppliers of funds to financial markets.

Financial flows are described as indirect finance if there is financial intermediation. Intermediation occurs when funds pass through financial institutions.

What distinguishes these institutions from other businesses is that securities dominate both sides of their balance sheet. They issue securities, which appear on the right-hand (or liability) side of their balance sheet. Funds obtained from selling these securities are then employed to purchase securities for the left-hand (or asset) side of their balance sheet.

If financial institutions are to operate with a profit, they must have a positive spread. The spread is the difference between two balance-sheet rates. It is the average rate that a financial institution earns on the securities they own (from the left-hand side of the balance sheet) minus the average rate that pay on debt securities that they issue (from the right-hand side of their balance sheet). For example, if the average return on a bank's assets is 5% and the average cost of its liabilities is 4%, the spread is 1%. The spread must be positive for a financial institution to be viable.

This raises an interesting issue. For a financial institution to operate successfully, it is apparent from Figure 3.2 that it must intercept the flow of funds from savings-surplus units to savings-deficit units. To operate with a positive spread, however, the financial institution must offer savings-surplus units a lower rate (on average) than they would obtain if they opted, instead, to purchase securities directly from savings-deficit units. The question, then, is: why would savings-surplus units agree to this arrangement?

The answer to this question provides insight into the operations of financial intermediaries. To induce savings-surplus units to purchase their securities with a lower average return, financial institutions must design financial instruments with distinct features that make them attractive to market participants. Investors must view these features favorably enough to cause them to purchase the securities even though they offer a lower average return. The growth and proliferation of financial institutions during the post-World War II period is testimony to their ability to accomplish this task.

The innovative features in the instruments offered by financial institutions are varied. Some instruments provide customers with favorable denominations. This is particularly true of depository institutions, where customers are able to deposit sums that vary anywhere from a few dollars to millions of dollars. Liquidity, too, is also an important feature, and depository institutions also offer instruments that are used as exchange media.

Many of the instruments offered by financial institutions allow owners to reduce their risk exposure. Deposits offered by banking institutions, for example, frequently carry insurance against default risk. Investment companies (or mutual funds) permit share owners to participate in the returns on a broadly diversified portfolio of securities. Life insurance companies insure against an untimely death by offering securities with death benefits.

Intertemporal Production and Exchange

The interest rate falls within the realm of intertemporal economics, or what Austrian theorist Eugen von Böhm-Bawerk called the "the present and future in economic life."[3] While the interest rate is not defined by everyone in the same way, it is useful to observe that the interest rate is intimately related to three intertemporal economic relationships: (1) the marginal productivity of capital; (2) the price of credit; and, (3) the marginal rate of time preference. Each of these phenomena has been employed in formulating a definition of the rate of interest. Understanding how these intertemporal phenomena are related to one another is central to the problem of defining the interest rate.

Marginal Productivity of Capital

Unlike land and labor, capital goods are the produced means of production. Moreover, they are produced for good reason. The production and use of capital goods, while necessarily more time-consuming (or "roundabout" according to Böhm-Bawerk), generally is productive. That is, the use of previously produced goods to produce additional goods generally results a net increase in the quantity of these goods. This net product, at the margin, is called the marginal productivity of capital (MP_K).

The productivity of capital goods raises the issue of how to describe this net product that results from their usage. Böhm-Bawerk referred to it as interest or, more specifically, *originary interest*. Interest in this sense is the payment to the input capital. Unless it is placed in the context of the intertemporal valuation of goods, however, this payment is likely to vanish (or go to zero). If individuals make no distinction (or are indifferent) between an equal quantity of goods now or goods in the future, they will tend to accumulate capital goods currently until the marginal product of capital is zero. At that point, capital accumulation ceases and the interest rate is zero.

Price of Credit

Individuals can give up their claims on current goods to others, and receive in exchange claims on future goods. Contracts specifying such exchanges are loan contracts, or bonds. The excess of future goods (if any) resulting from this intertemporal exchange is also commonly called interest (or the interest rate when expressed in proportionate terms).[4]

Borrowers who issue these bonds are renting the use of money for a specified period of time. Thus, when used in this context, the interest rate is a rental payment for the use of borrowed funds. This rate is frequently described, alternatively, as the price of credit.

The price of credit, likewise, will tend to vanish unless it is placed in the context of the intertemporal valuation of goods. If individuals make no distinction (or are indifferent) between an equal quantity of goods now or goods in the future, they will readily exchange present and future goods with one another on equal terms. The price of credit in this case is zero.[5]

Marginal Rate of Time Preference

The phenomenon that keeps the marginal productivity of capital and the price of credit from potentially going to zero is time preferences. These subjective preferences represent how individuals value goods now relative to goods in the future, or present consumption relative to future consumption.

The marginal rate of time preference (MRTP) is a quantitative expression of these valuations for incremental units. It is the quantity of future goods an individual is willing to sacrifice for a specified quantity of present goods of comparable quality. It is normally formulated in proportionate terms, as in equation 3.10. If MRTP = 5%, for example, an individual is indifferent between a given quantity of present goods and 5% more future goods.

$$MRTP = |dC_1/dC_0| - 1 \qquad (3.10)$$

where dC_1 and dC_0 are changes in future goods (or consumption) and present goods, respectively. The ratio of these changes is an absolute value.

An individual who prefers present goods over future goods is said to have positive time preferences, i.e., MRTP > 0. One who is indifferent has neutral time preferences (MRTP = 0), and one who prefers future goods over present goods, negative time preferences (MRTP < 0).

Individuals are generally viewed as having positive time references. If that is the case, then the marginal productivity of capital and the price of credit need not vanish. The case of a positive price for credit (or interest) is considered below in the discussion of the real interest rate. The case for a positive marginal productivity of capital is discussed presently.

In the absence of a credit (and/or equity) market, all capital formation is internally financed. That is, all capital goods are financed through the saving of the economic unit accumulating capital goods. Each unit must weigh the value of current goods sacrificed against the value of the additional future goods resulting from the employment of those capital goods. With positive time preferences, the unit will accumulate capital goods (currently) up to the point where the marginal productivity of capital is equal to the marginal rate of time preference.

$$MP_K = MRTP > 0 \qquad (3.11)$$

If the marginal productivity of capital were to exceed the marginal rate of time preference ($MP_K > MRTP$), the individual will choose to further abstain from present consumption and accumulate more capital goods. Assume for example that the MP_K is 6% and the MRTP is 5%. This individual would be indifferent between a given quantity of present goods and 5% more future goods. However, abstaining from present goods and accumulating capital goods results in 6% more future goods. The individual is clearly better off accumulating more capital goods, and will continue to do so until the equality in equation 3.11 is obtained. By similar reasoning, the individual will accumulate fewer capital goods whenever the marginal productivity of capital is less than the marginal rate of time preference, again until 3.11 is obtained. It is important to note that, in both cases, the marginal productivity of capital conforms to the positive rate of time preferences.

Defining Interest

While there is general agreement concerning the intertemporal nature of interest, there is no such general agreement about the definition of the interest rate. It has been defined as the return to the input capital and, alternatively, as the price of credit. Ludwig von Mises defined it yet another way: as the rate of time preference.[6]

There is good reason for defining interest in the manner of von Mises. It was noted above that both the return to capital and the price of credit tend to vanish (or go to zero) in the absence of positive time preferences. That is, both of these phenomena rest on the pillars of time preference. Moreover, both are simply different manifestations of how individuals are willing to exchange future goods for present goods.

For those reasons, defining interest as the rate of time preference is preferred. This expression is general enough to encompass different forms of intertemporal exchange such as credit transactions and the return to capital. As discussed below, this definition of interest can also be modified to accommodate the possibility of contract default in intertemporal exchanges.

In conventional parlance, however, the interest rate is most often discussed not as the rate of time preference, but as the price of credit. This is true in the world of finance, and particularly in discussions of money and monetary policy. While less preferred for the reasons just noted, on grounds of expediency that expression for interest is subsequently employed.

Interest Rates

The Real Interest Rate

The interest rate can be expressed either in nominal or real terms. The nominal (or money) interest rate is the price of credit expressed in terms of money. The real interest rate, sometimes referred to as the "pure" rate of interest, is the price of credit expressed in terms of physical units (or goods and services).

When markets are free, borrowers and lenders determine the price of credit. It is anticipated that these economic agents will act rationally, that is, that they will think in real terms. (Those who do not are said to suffer from "money illusion.") It follows that, for such rational decision-makers, it is the real interest rate that influences their choices.

This makes the analysis of credit markets somewhat subtle, because the real interest rate generally is not observable. What we typically observe is the nominal rate of interest. The nominal rate is the one typically quoted in the financial media, and generally it is the rate explicitly negotiated in credit contracts. This means that economic agents think in real terms, but most often negotiate credit contracts in nominal terms.

The Positive Real Rate of Interest

With few exceptions, those who attempt to estimate the real interest rate obtain a positive number. A fundamental analytical issue, then, is explaining this empirical outcome—that the real rate of interest is positive. The theory advanced to account for this phenomenon is the existence of positive time preferences for consumption. As noted above, time preferences are concerned with how individuals value goods now relative to an equivalent amount of goods in the future (or present consumption relative to future consumption). An individual who prefers present consumption to future consumption is said to have positive time preferences. By contrast, one who is indifferent has neutral time preferences; one who prefers future consumption, negative time preferences.

If sufficient number of individuals have zero time preferences, the real interest rate will be zero. Those who wish to borrow in the credit market are able to obtain additional claims on current goods from lenders with zero time preferences. These lenders are indifferent between current consumption and future consumption, and willingly give up their claims to current goods in exchange for claims to an equal quantity of future goods. That is, they do so at a zero interest rate. Compensation in the form of a positive real interest rate is unnecessary because of their indifference between present and future consumption.

This is shown graphically in Figure 3.3. The supply curve for loanable funds follows the quantity axis. No matter what the demand for loanable funds, the real interest rate remains zero. Graphically, as the demand for loanable funds shifts from D_0 to D_1 to D_2, the supply of loanable funds is perfectly elastic at the zero rate of interest.

On the other hand, if a significant number of individuals have positive time preferences, the real interest rate will be positive. Now, individuals borrowing (in the credit market) to acquire more current goods must pay a positive real interest rate. The reason is that lenders with positive time preferences will not give up their claims on current goods unless they are compensated.

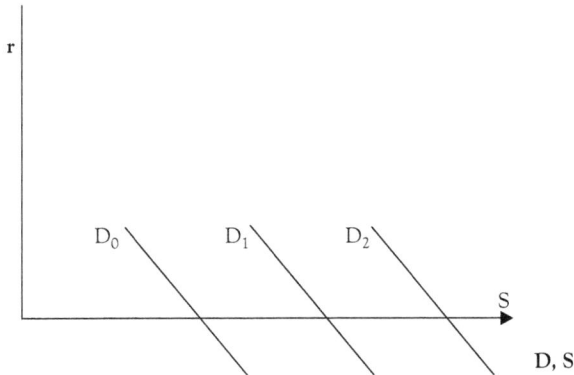

Figure 3.3 Market for loanable funds

It is in this way that positive time preferences account for the existence of a positive real interest rate. Moreover, this real rate is a precise expression of those time preferences. Hence, the real interest rate is referred to as the rate of time preference. A 5% real interest rate, for example, indicates that individuals are willing to sacrifice present consumption if they are compensated by 5% additional future consumption.

Level of the Real Interest Rate

A graph of the loanable funds market is presented in Figure 3.4. Both sides of the market reflect the time preferences of market participants. The supply curve is a locus of points showing the willingness of economic agents to forego present consumption at different interest rates. A higher real interest rate represents a larger compensation for deferring present consumption. Consequently, more funds are supplied at higher real interest rates.

The demand side of the market for loanable funds also reflects time preferences. Borrowers in this market obtain claims for present consumption from lenders. Some borrowers may be consumers desirous of consuming in excess of their income, i.e., dissaving. Others may be businesses wanting to finance the acquisition of additional capital goods by borrowing.

Borrowers must sacrifice future consumption in order to obtain claims for present consumption. The amount of the sacrifice is specified by the real rate of interest, which indicates the rate of exchange of future

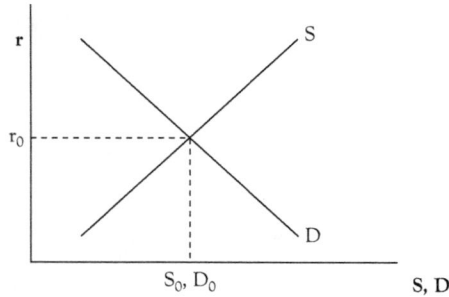

Figure 3.4 Market for loanable funds

consumption for present consumption. With a smaller sacrifice (i.e., the lower the real interest rate), more funds are demanded by borrowers.

Price plays an allocative role in this market. The real interest rate allocates available funds among alternative users. At the equilibrium interest rate, r_0, the quantity of loanable funds demanded is equal to the quantity supplied. The disparate plans of all market participants are rendered consistent with one another. It is adjustments in the real interest rate that brings about this consistency of plans.

When the plans of all economic agents are consistent with one another (at interest rate r_0), resources in the economy are allocated in such a manner that aggregate saving is equal to aggregate investment ($S = I$). All resources released by those abstaining from present consumption are absorbed in the production of capital goods. These capital goods, in turn, are available for the future production of consumables.

As an expression of time preferences, the real interest rate is the market assessment of how economic agents are willing to exchange present and future consumption. When these time preferences change, so, too, does the real interest rate. Assume, for example, that there are reduced time preferences for present consumption. This can take several forms. Some individuals with positive saving may choose to save more. The result is a rightward shift in the supply curve of loanable funds (from S_0 to S_1 in Figure 3.5, left panel).

Another possibility is that individuals previously dissaving choose to dissave less. In this case, the demand for loanable funds decreases and the demand curve shifts to the left (from D_0 to D_1 in the left panel).

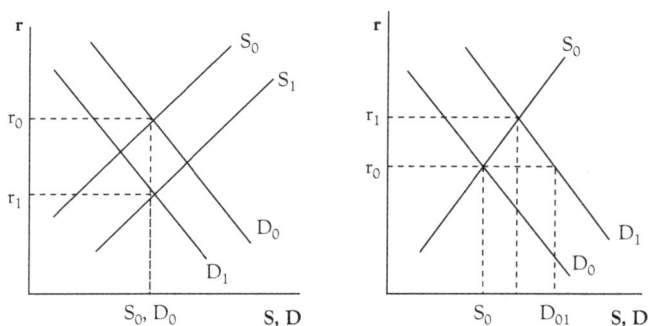

Figure 3.5 Market for loanable funds

A third possibility is that there is a combination of the two. That is what is depicted in Figure 3.5, left panel. The supply of loanable funds increases and the demand decreases. At the previously prevailing interest rate (r_0), there is now an excess supply of loanable funds. Competition among suppliers results in a decline in the equilibrium real interest rate. The new market clearing rate is r_1.

Changes in the perceived marginal productivity of capital also cause time preferences to change. An increase in the productivity of capital, for example, increases business demand for capital goods. Capital goods are present goods, and this constitutes an increase in time preferences for current goods. The result is an increase in the demand for loanable funds. In Figure 3.5, right panel, the demand curve for loanble funds shifts to the right (from $\mathbf{D_0}$ to $\mathbf{D_1}$). At the previously-prevailing real interest rate, r_0, there is now excess demand for loanable funds. Competition among those seeking claims to current consumption forces the real interest rate upward. The market clears at interest rate r_1.

Risk and the Real Rate of Interest

Analysis of the real interest rate to this point has neglected risk factors.[7] The "pure" interest rate was a risk-free rate. The introduction of risk can affect the level of the real interest rate because risk-averse lenders must be compensated for the risk that they incur as suppliers of funds to financial markets.

There are several types of potential risk that are of importance to market participants. Two are default risk and price risk. Default risk is the risk that the borrower will not repay funds that are advanced by lenders. If that occurs, the lender incurs financial loss. Given this possibility, borrowers generally must compensate lenders by offering a risk premium in the real rate.

Price risk, on the other hand, is the risk that the price of a debt security will vary during the holding period. It has significance to investors because they often do not know with certainty when the security will be liquidated. Selling a security whose price has fallen substantially results in a sizable capital loss. As a consequence, this type of risk, too, can give rise to a risk premium in the real interest rate.

The size of the risk premium, if any, in the real interest rate is dependent upon the risk preferences of market participants. For those who are risk-averse, less risk is preferred to more risk. If investors generally exhibit such preferences, the real rate will include a risk premium that embodies the market valuation of the risk involved.[8] Greater risk is associated with a higher risk premium (and a higher real interest rate); less risk, with a lower risk premium (and a lower real rate).

Although we are unable to directly observe the preferences of market participants, rate patterns in the marketplace generally are consistent with risk-averse behavior as described above. The dominance of this type of behavior has significance beyond affecting the level of the real interest rate. With risk-averse behavior, the real interest rate no longer represents the rate of time preference for both borrowers and lenders. There is now a wedge between their time preferences in the amount of the risk premium.

This situation is graphically shown in Figure 3.6, where the loanable funds market in the presence of risk is compared to the same market when there is no risk. Consider, initially, the case with no risk. The supply and demand for loanable funds are represented by curves **S** and **D**, respectively. With price playing its customary rationing role, the loanable funds market clears at interest rate r_1. This real interest rate represents the time preferences of both lenders and borrowers. At this rate, the quantity demanded of loanable funds (D_1) is equal to the quantity supplied (S_1).

Once risk is introduced, risk-averse lenders will require compensation for the risk they incur. Compensation occurs because they are less will-

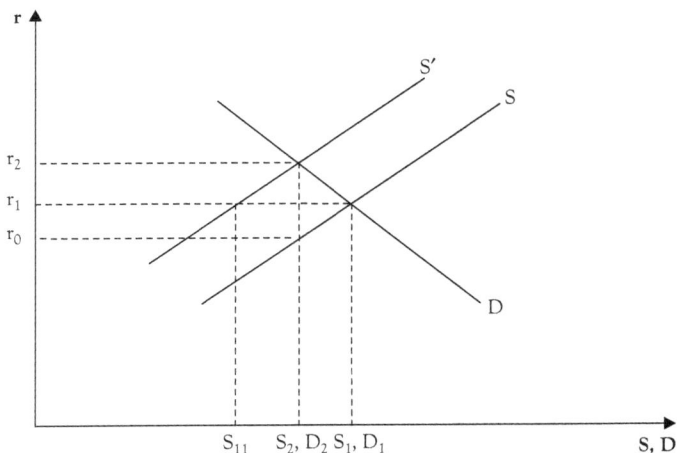

Figure 3.6 Market for loanable funds

ing to lend than they were before. This is manifested in a leftward shift in the supply curve for loanable funds (from S to S'). For each quantity of loanable funds supplied, the real interest rate is now higher. At the previous equilibrium interest rate (r_1), there is now an excess demand for loanable funds ($D_1 - S_{11}$). Competition among borrowers drives the real rate higher to its new equilibrium level, r_2. The quantities of loanable funds supplied and demanded are now S_2 and D_2.

This new equilibrium interest rate (r_2) is an expression of the time preferences of borrowers. It represents how much future consumption they are willing to sacrifice in order to consume more currently. r_2, however, does not represent the time preferences of lenders. Instead, it represents the summation of the time preferences of lenders (r_0) and the necessary risk premium ($r_2 - r_0$) given their risk-averse behavior.

In the absence of risk, lenders will supply a lower quantity of funds, S_2, at rate r_0 (a movement down supply curve **S**) than they would at r_1. The rate r_0 now represents their tradeoff of present and future consumption, or their time preferences. In the presence of risk, a risk premium ($r_2 - r_0$) is added to their rate of time preference, and lenders supply the same quantity of funds, S_2, at the higher real rate r_2. The risk premium now constitutes a wedge between the time preferences of borrowers and lenders.

The Nominal Interest Rate

The nominal interest rate is the price of credit expressed in monetary units. Most interest rate quotes are nominal rates. Three features of those nominal rates are discussed below. First, the nominal interest rate is related to bond prices. Second, the nominal interest rate is affected by inflationary expectations. Finally, the characteristics of bonds vary. As a consequence, there is not a single nominal rate, but rather an entire vector of nominal interest rates.

Bond Prices and Interest Rates

Bonds traded in financial markets represent borrowed funds. They are issued by borrowers and purchased by lenders. Associated with each bond is a price and an interest rate. Bond prices are an expression of the subjective value of the bonds to traders in the market. These valuations change and, as a consequence, so do bond prices.

Those issuing bonds usually are renting the use of money for a specified period of time. The rental payment for these funds is the interest rate, or the price of credit. Having stated this, it is important to state what the interest rate is not. The interest rate is not the price of money, as is sometimes claimed. The price of money, as noted above, is its exchange value relative to other things. Assuming that P is the average price of other things, then the purchasing power of money (or the price of money) is the reciprocal of P (see pp. 7–8 above).

Many bonds are actively traded in the secondary (or resale) market. In the secondary market, bond prices and nominal (or money) interest rates are inversely related. This occurs because the nominal interest rate for newly issued (or primary) debt constantly changes. Market traders respond to variations in the interest rate by revaluing previously issued bonds. This revaluation is necessary for previously issued debt securities to remain price-competitive with the newly issued debt.

An example of this kind of revaluation is presented in Exhibit 3.1. The bond traded is a perpetuity, i.e., it has no maturation date. The borrower issues the bond in Period 1 with a price of $1,000. The coupon payment of $50 is sufficient to induce lenders to purchase the bond. With

Period	Bond price	Coupon	Interest
1	$1,000	$50	5%
2	$500	$50	10%

Exhibit 3.1 Bond Prices and Interest Rates

this coupon payment, the bond owners receive 5 percent nominal interest on this investment.

In Period 2, market conditions change. The nominal interest rate on newly issued debt increases to 10%. The individuals who purchased perpetuities in period 1 continue to receive an annual interest (or coupon) payment of $50. If they choose to sell their bonds in Period 2, however, they will have to do so at a lower price. No one will pay them the $1,000 they initially paid for the bonds. At that price, those purchasing these perpetuities would only receive an interest rate of 5%. This is below the 10% rate they would receive when purchasing newly issued debt securities.

However, investors would be willing to purchase these perpetuities on the secondary market at a lower price. At a price of $500, the interest rate they would receive when purchasing these securities on the secondary market is equal to the 10% return on newly issued bonds. That is, $50/$500 = 10%. Thus, the price of the perpetuities falls to $500.

This example was for an increase in the nominal interest rate. If the nominal rate were to fall, the opposite occurs. Bond prices increase. In general, when the nominal interest rate changes in financial markets, prices of previously issued bonds in those markets move in the opposite direction.

Inflationary Expectations

The study of the relationship between the nominal and real interest rates draws upon the work of Irving Fisher. It is possible for these two rates to be the same. That is not the case, however, in an inflationary environment. Because the world of fiat money is a world of inflation, Fisher's analysis of how bond traders adjust bond prices and interest rates in response to changes in inflation has assumed much greater importance.

Equation 3.12 below is known as the Fisher equation. It shows the relationship between nominal and real rates of interest, and how they are affected by inflation.

$$i = r + (dP/P)^*$$
(3.12)

where i is the nominal interest,
r is the real interest rate, and
(dP/P)* is the expected rate of change of the average price during the term of the credit contract.

Credit contracts are *ex ante* relationships. Any inflation that occurs during the term of the contract will erode the purchasing power of the money loaned. Borrowers will repay lenders in monetary units that have less purchasing power than the money they borrowed. This affects the real wealth of both borrowers and lenders. As a consequence, rational economic agents (on both sides of the contract) must take inflation into account when entering credit contracts.

When credit contracts are consummated, the actual rate of inflation during the term of a contract is not known. What affects contracts, then, are the inflationary expectations of borrowers and lenders. According to Fisher, the expected rate of inflation [dP/P)*] is fully incorporated into terms of credit contracts—in the form of a higher nominal rate of interest. This is how the borrower compensates the lender for expected changes in the purchasing power of the money during the term of the contract.

This compensation appears as the last term in the Fisher equation [dP/P)*]. It is known as the inflation premium in the credit contract. Note that when expected inflation goes up, so too, does the nominal rate of interest. When inflationary expectations decline, the nominal rate falls commensurately.

These adjustments in the level of the nominal rate of interest are a market phenomenon. It is the way that borrowers and lenders respond to changes in the inflationary environment. When inflation increases, the purchasing power of the money loaned depreciates more rapidly. Lenders would like additional compensation in the form of a higher interest rate.

A higher interest rate, however, is not in the self-interest of borrowers. What motivates them to offer a higher rate is the competition for available funds in credit markets. With higher inflation, many assets are increasing in value. The price of farm land, for example, may rise from $2,500 per acre to $3,000 and then $4,000 per acre. Owners of assets that are appreciating in value are willing to bid up the price of credit because the assets they are purchasing with borrowed money are gaining in value.

An example of how participants in credit markets adapt to different inflationary environments is presented in Exhibit 3.2. In Case I, market participants expect price stability. As a consequence, the nominal and real rates are the same (3%). Assume individual A lends $100 to individual B for one year. At the end of the contract period, B pays A, $103. The payment consists of $100 in principal and $3 in interest. If inflationary expectations were correct, the $100 in principal will purchase the same quantity of goods at both the beginning and end of the contract period. Moreover, the $103 received by A will purchase 3% more goods and services than the $100 loaned. Thus, not only is the nominal rate of interest 3%, but the real rate is 3% as well.

The world changes, and inflation increases. This affects expectations. In Case II, borrowers and lenders now anticipate 10% annual inflation. These higher inflationary expectations are incorporated into the terms of credit contracts. The nominal rate of interest increases from 3% to 13%. The difference, of course, is the higher inflation premium.

Now individual A loans individual B $100. One year later, B repays the loan with interest, or $113. Assuming expectations are correct, the $100 in principal returned will purchase 10% fewer goods and services than when the loan was made. The inflation premium of 10%, however, compensates the lender for this erosion in the purchasing power of the principal. That is, $10 of the $13 in nominal interest represents this

Case	i	r	(dP/P)*
I	3	3	0
II	13	3	10

Exhibit 3.2 The Fisher equation

compensation to the lender. $110 (of the $113) received by the lender will now purchase the same quantity of goods and services as the $100 initially loaned. What remains is $3 in interest. That $3 is the real interest rate in this example. The $113 received by the lender will purchase 3% more goods and services than the $100 initially loaned in this contract.

This market adjustment is shown graphically in Figure 3.7. In the market for loanable funds, the vertical axis is the nominal interest rate; the horizontal axis, the quantity of loanable funds. Initial equilibrium occurs at the nominal interest rate i_I (or 3%). This corresponds to Case I in Exhibit 3.2. With expectations of zero inflation, the real rate of interest is also 3%.

In Case II, inflationary expectations increase to 10%. Each nominal interest rate on the vertical axis now corresponds to a lower real interest rate. For example, the 3% nominal rate now corresponds to a real interest rate of negative 7% (versus a plus 3% before). As a consequence, lenders will want to lend less at each nominal interest rate. Borrowers will want to borrow more at each nominal rate.

These changes appear graphically as a leftward shift in the supply curve (from S_I to S_{II}), and a rightward shift in the demand curve (from D_I to D_{II}). The previously prevailing equilibrium rate of interest rate (3%) no longer clears the credit market. There is excess demand at this

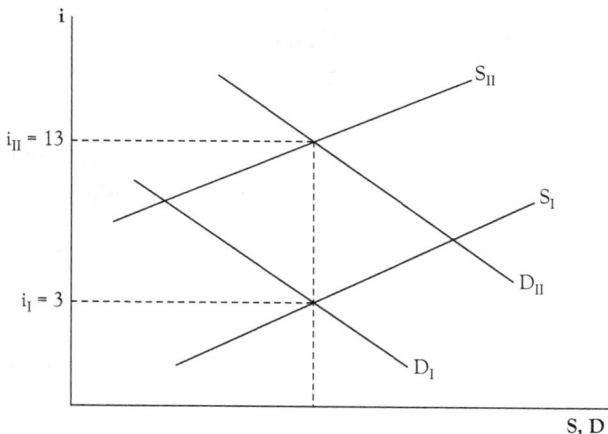

Figure 3.7 **Market for loanable funds**

rate. Competition among borrowers for available funds causes the nominal rate of interest to move higher. At the 13% nominal rate, the credit market again clears. This nominal rate now corresponds to a 3% real interest rate. The market for loanable funds clears at the same real rate as before.

Fisher's analysis, then, shows how open credit markets accommodate inflation. Although there are numerous empirical studies of Fisher's theory, two observations are cited here to demonstrate how the theory often conforms to the data. First, the U.S mortgage rate recently fell below 4%. This is much lower than the rate in the early 1980s, which was nearly 17%. What would account for such a dramatic fall in the nominal rate of interest? Fisher's analysis would suggest that the inflation rate in the early 1980s must have been considerably higher. Indeed, it was. The consumer price index (CPI) rose by 13.5% in 1980; in 2012, only 2.1%.

A second observation is that nominal interest rates vary substantially across countries. Based on Fisher's analysis, countries with relatively low inflation should have relatively low nominal rates of interest. Alternatively, relatively high inflation countries should have correspondingly higher nominal rates of interest. That, too, generally is the case.

A final issue addressed here has to do with forecasting errors. In the previous examples, it was assumed that expectations were correct, that is, there were no forecasting errors. In those cases, $(dP/P)^* = dP/P$. Expected inflation is equal to actual inflation or, alternatively, *ex ante* inflation is equal to *ex post* inflation.

Most often, there are forecasting errors. Such errors are important because they result in transfers of wealth. The nature of the transfer depends on whether market participants forecast the inflation rate too high or too low. When they forecast it too high [$(dP/P)^* > dP/P$], wealth is transferred from borrowers to lenders. When $(dP/P)^* < dP/P$, the opposite occurs. Wealth is transferred from lenders to borrowers.

Examples of both types of transfer are presented in Exhibit 3.3. Case I is the credit contract. It is an *ex ante* relationship, with a nominal interest rate of 8%. The expected rate of inflation during the term of the contract is 5%. Given these expectations, the anticipated real rate of interest is 3%.

Cases II and III are two different *ex post* scenarios. In Case II, the actual rate of inflation during the term of the contract was 10%. This was

Case	i	r	(dP/P)*	dP/P
I: *ex ante*	8	3	5	–
II: *ex post*	8	-2	–	10
III: *ex post*	8	8	–	0

Exhibit 3.3 Wealth Transfers

higher than expected $[(dP/P)^* < dP/P]$. Market participants anticipated a real interest rate of 3%, but the actual (*ex post*) real rate was a negative 2%. This unexpected lower real rate benefited borrowers at the expense of lenders. Had lenders known that the real interest rate was going to be negative 2%, they never would have entered the contract. Had borrowers known, they would have borrowed much more.

This forecasting error transferred wealth across the credit contract from lenders to borrowers. The form of the transfer was the lower real interest rate. Enormous amounts of wealth have been transferred in this way.

A recent historical example occurred in the United States in the 1970s and early 1980s. Inflation accelerated sharply. As a consequence, actual inflation rates rose above anticipated rates of inflation. While borrowers were feeling very good about long-term loan contracts consummated in the 1960s, lenders were not. Indeed, this forecasting error caused many lenders to declare bankruptcy. Among them were numerous banks and savings and loan associations. So severe was the problem that the U.S. government deemed it politically desirable to funnel large quantities of tax dollars into failing financial institutions.

In Case III, the actual rate of inflation (0%) is lower than expected inflation. This situation benefits lenders (at the expense of borrowers). The *ex ante* real interest rate was 3%. The *ex post* real rate was 8%. Many borrowers would have refused to enter credit contracts had they known the real interest rate was going to be this high.

The wealth transfer, in this case, is from borrowers to lenders. It is in the form of a higher than expected real rate of interest. The United

States experienced this situation in the 1980s, when the rate of inflation decelerated sharply. Many borrowers declared bankruptcy. This included farmers, agricultural equipment dealers, and building contractors.

Farmers who borrowed to acquire more land expected that land values would appreciate (as they had when inflation accelerated in the 1970s). They anticipated repaying the loans by selling commodities at higher prices (again, like the 1970s). These events did not come to pass.

A similar fate befell building contractors. Many borrowed to construct houses prior to selling them. This market tactic had "worked" for much of the 1970s. When the anticipated rise in housing prices did not materialize, expected profits turned to losses.

In a very general sense, Fisher's interest-rate model is yet another testimony to the resiliency of markets. Through nuances in prices, markets transmit all kinds of information. In this case, the information transmitted in bond markets is the expected rate of inflation. This analysis has been especially useful in our contemporary world of fiat money, where inflation rates largely have been positive and often quite volatile. In those cases where governments have not arbitrarily fixed interest rates, Fisher's analysis shows the adaptation that occurs in financial markets in response to the vagaries of inflation.

The Vector of Nominal Interest Rates

Hitherto, the discussion has focused on a single interest rate—*the* rate of interest. That simplification facilitated discussion of the market for debt securities. In reality, there are many different interest rates. This is reflected in the interest rate vector in 3.13, where there are n different nominal interest rates. Individual rates in this vector might represent the interest rate on federal funds, 3-month Treasury bills, 6-month Treasury bills, 10-year Treasury bonds, corporate bonds, mortgages, 6-month certificates of deposit, and rates on numerous other debt securities.

$$(i_1, i_2, i_3, i_4, i_5, \ldots i_n) \tag{3.13}$$

Debt securities have different interest rates because they are not identical, i.e., they have different characteristics. Interest-rate differentials such as those in 3.13 reflect market pricing of these characteristics. Many of these characteristics were discussed earlier in the chapter. One example is inflationary expectations and their impact on nominal interest rates. Expected inflation for the next six months may differ from expected inflation for the next two years. Both of these may differ from expected inflation for the next 10 years. Because debt securities vary by maturity, the inflation premium will not be the same for securities of different maturity. This may account for a portion of the interest rate differences in equation 3.13.

Interest rates in vector 3.13 may also vary because securities do not all have the same risk characteristics. Nuances in risk are priced into securities by market participants. An example is default risk, which can vary considerably across loan contracts. Differences in default risk may reflect the fact that individual borrowers face different financial environments. Borrowers may also warrant different rates if they have different ethical standards regarding the repayment of debt.

A case where default risk is considered relatively low is debt securities issued by the U.S. government. Like other national governments, the U.S. government has an advantage over other borrowers because it has the power to both tax and print money. Moreover, the U.S. government has a record of not defaulting on its credit contracts. As a result of these factors, market participants generally consider it very unlikely that the U.S. government will default on its debt obligations. That makes it possible for the U.S. government to borrow at relatively low nominal interest rates. By contrast, most other borrowers pay higher rates. At the other end of the risk spectrum from U.S. government securities are pay-day loans and loans at pawn shops. Default risk and interest rates are much higher for these securities.

Other factors that occasion variations in nominal interest rates include tax features and time preferences. Intergovernmental relations result in some securities having a more favorable tax status. Interest on state and local government securities, for example, generally is exempt from federal income taxes. Interest on U.S. government securities, in turn, is exempt from state income taxes. Because investors are interested in after-tax income, such differences in tax treatments are incorporated into bond prices and rates.

Time preferences have an impact because it is unlikely that the willingness of individuals to trade-off current consumption for consumption one year from now is the same as their willingness to trade-off current consumption for consumption five years, ten years, or twenty years from now. If that is the case, differences in time preferences will also account for some of the interest-rate variations observed in equation 3.13.

The Term Structure of Interest Rates

Not only do interest rates differ at a given point in time, but returns on securities can vary based on differences in their maturity. A curve showing the yields of a set of securities differing only in maturity is known as the term structure of interest rates, or the yield curve. Each point on the curve is an ordered pair, and associates the maturity of a security with its yield. While it is not easy to find actual situations where securities differ only in their maturity, a popular rendition is to show the different yields on securities issued by the U.S. Treasury.

Analysis of the term structure of interest rates is related to explaining its shape. Three yield curves with differing shapes are presented in Figure 3.8. The yield curve in Panel (a) is horizontal. With a horizontal yield curve, security yields do not vary by maturity. The yield on a six-month security is the same as the yield on one-year, two-year, three-year, and ten-year securities.

The yield curve in Panel (b) is ascending. With an ascending yield curve, the yield increases with the time to maturity. Hence, the yield on a six-month security is less than the yield on a one-year security which, in turn, is lower than the yield on a two-year security. From an empirical standpoint, the yield curve most often assumes this form. Consequently, the ascending yield curve is sometimes referred to as the normal yield curve.

The term structure depicted in Panel (c) occurs much less frequently. Referred to as a descending yield curve, it is more likely to happen when inflation is relatively high.

For a descending yield curve, the yield on a six-month security is higher than the yield on a one-year security which, in turn, is higher than the yield on a two-year security. Yields on three-year, five-year, and ten-year securities are sequentially lower.[9]

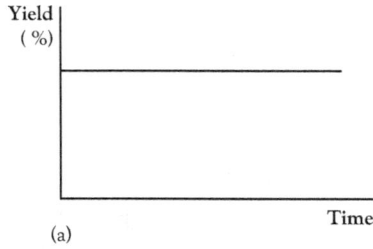

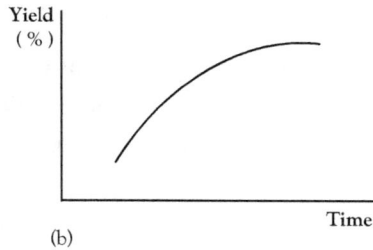

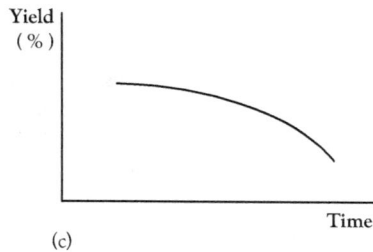

Figure 3.8 The term structures of interest rates.

Forward Rates

Implicit in any term structure of interest rates is a set of forward rates. These rates are not actual interest rates. Instead, they implied reinvestment rates. They are rates that would have to prevail if a sequence of investments in short-term securities is to have the same over all return as the return on a long-term security. The sum of the maturities for the short-term securities must equal the maturity of the long-term security.

Assume, for example, that bond A matures in one year and bond B matures in three years. The forward rate (in this case) is the interest rate on a two-year bond, available one year from now, that causes the compounded yield on the one-year bond (A) and two-year bond to equal to the compounded yield on the three-year bond (B). Thus, the proceeds from owning the one-year bond and investing the proceeds (at maturity) in the two-year bond are identical to the proceeds from owning the three-year bond. Equation 3.14 expresses this relationship symbolically.

$$(1 + {}_tR_3)^3 = (1 + {}_tR_1)(1 + {}_{t+1}r_2)^2 \qquad (3.14)$$

where ${}_tR_3$ is the current nominal (or spot) rate on a three-year bond,

${}_tR_1$ is the current nominal rate on a one-year bond, and

${}_{t+1}r_2$ is the annual forward rate on a two-year security available one year from now.

Inserting numeric values, assume that the one year nominal rate is 4% (${}_tR_1 = 4\%$) and the three-year rate is 5% (${}_tR_3 = 5\%$). The implicit two-year forward rate in this case is 5.504%, i.e., ${}_{t+1}r_2 = 5.504\%$.

Forward rates such as this one are strictly mathematical calculations. They assume importance, however, because they are given behavioral content in current explanations of the term structure of interest rates. Three alternative theories of the term structure are presented below.[10]

Unbiased Expectations Theory

This theory relies upon expectations to account for differences in yields for securities that differ only in their maturity.[11] Each interest rate in a given term structure of interest rates is determined by expected future interest rates. Moreover, these expected future interest rates are operational. It is possible to compute them because forward rates have important informational content. According to the unbiased expectations theory, each forward rate implicit in the term structure is an unbiased estimate of the expected future interest rate for that same period.

With ρ representing the expected future interest rate, this relationship between forward rates and expected future interest rates is presented in equations 3.15 and 3.16. In 3.15, the forward rate for a j-year security available i years from now (${}_{t+i}r_j$) is equal to the expected interest rate on the j-year security available i years from now (${}_{t+i}\rho_j$). The unbiased nature of the forward rate is exhibited by differencing the two rates, as in 3.16.

$$_{t+i}r_j = {}_{t+i}\rho_j \qquad\qquad (3.15)$$

$$_{t+i}r_j - {}_{t+i}\rho_j = 0 \qquad\qquad (3.16)$$

To further illustrate the relationship between forward rates and expected future interest rates, consider equation 3.17. Because all forward rates are of the form $_{t+i}r_1$, each is a one-year forward rate. According to the unbiased expectations theory, the forward rate on a one-year security available one year from now ($_{t+1}r_1$) is the estimate of the expected interest rate for a one-year security available one year from now ($_{t+1}\rho_1$). $_{t+2}r_1$, in turn, serves as the estimate of the expected interest rate on a one-year bond available two years from now ($_{t+2}\rho_1$). A similar interpretation is attached to the other forward rates. It follows that the long-term rate under consideration ($_tR_n$) is determined by this set of expected future interest rates.

$$(1 + {}_tR_n)^n = (1 + {}_tR_1)\,(1 + {}_{t+1}r_1)\,(1 + {}_{t+2}r_1) \ldots (1 + {}_{t+n-1}r_1) \qquad (3.17)$$

where $_tR_n$ is the current (or spot) interest rate on an n-year bond at time t, and

$_{t+i}r_1$ is the forward rate on a one-year bond at time t + i.

The cogency of this argument about the nature of forward rates is not contingent upon the fact that all forward rates in 3.17 are one-year rates. Forward rates could have any maturity less than or equal to n−1. What is germane about the argument, however, is that it generalizes to all nominal rates for a given term structure of interest rates. That is, each current interest rate on the yield curve is determined by expected future interest rates. That is the essence of the unbiased expectations theory.

The proposition that current interest rates are determined by expected future interest rates begs the question about determinants of expected future interest rates. While the unbiased expectations theory does not directly address this issue, one would anticipate that factors influencing expected future rates would not differ from those affecting the level of the current interest rate. If that is correct, then phenomena such as time preferences for consumption and expected inflation influence the shape of the yield curve. Default risk and money risk, however, largely do not. The reason is that the unbiased expectations theory generally presumes that the activities of bond traders squeeze risk premiums out of the term structure of interest rates.

There are three important implications of the unbiased expectations theory. First, expectations about future interest rates determine current interest rates. The current yield on a long-term bond is a geometric average of the current yield on a short-term bond and expected yields on a series of sequential short-term bonds whose maturities sum to the maturity of the long-term bond. In equation 3.17, for example, the long-term interest rate $(_tR_n)$, is a geometric average of the one-year spot rate $(_tR_1)$ and the expected interest rates for a sequence of n−1 separate one-year bonds. The maturities of these short-term bonds sum to n, the maturity of the long-term bond.

A second implication of the unbiased expectations theory is that the significance of maturity diminishes for the bond investor. If one considers an n-year investment period, the expected return is the same whether one purchases an n-year bond or a series of shorter term bonds and reinvests the proceeds. One such set of possibilities is presented in Figure 3.9. The compounded return with investment plan A is $(1 + {_tR_n})^n$. In this case, the investor purchases an n-year bond. For plan B, the investor purchases an n−1 year bond and invests the proceeds (at maturity) for one year. In plan C, the investor purchases an n−2 year bond and, at maturity, purchases sequentially two one-year bonds.

Investment plan	Compounded return
A	$(1 + {_tR_n})^n$
B	$(1 + {_tR_{n-1}})^{n-1} (1 + {_{t+n-1}r_1})$
C	$(1 + {_tR_{n-2}})^{n-2} (1 + {_{t+n-2}r_1}) (1 + {_{t+n-1}r_1})$
.	
.	
.	
n	$(1 + {_tR_1}) (1 + {_{t+1}r_1}) (1 + {_{t+2}r_1}) .... (1 + {_{t+n-1}r_1})$

Figure 3.9 Returns on an n-year investment

In the final case, the investor purchases a sequential series of one-year bonds. With forward rates serving as unbiased estimates of expected future rates, the expected return for all n of these investment plans is the same. The maturity of the instruments selected has no bearing on the investor's expected n-period return.

A final implication of the unbiased expectations theory is that it provides an explanation for variously shaped yield curves. For a horizontal yield curve [as in Figure 3.8, panel (a)], the level of the interest rate is not expected to change. With expected future rates the same as the current short-term rate, the average of these expected rates is identical to the current short-rate.

An ascending yield curve [Figure 3.8, panel (b)] implies that bond traders expect interest rates to rise in the future. That is necessary if the geometric average of these expected future rates is above the current short-term rate. One thing that could occasion such a pattern of expected future rates is inflationary expectations, e.g., if investors expected future inflation to be higher than current inflation.

Finally, descending yield curves, which are empirically rare, occur when investors expect interest rates to fall. This normally happens when interest rates are relatively high (by historical standards). In this situation, the expectation that rates would return to more normal levels would give rise to a negatively sloped yield curve.

One of the principal weaknesses of the unbiased expectations theory is that it assumes that transactions costs are unimportant. That is necessary if forward rates are to serve as unbiased expectations of expected future interest rates. For, if transactions costs are important, they constitute a portion of each forward rate. In this case, forward rates are higher than expected future interest rates. That is, they are (upward) biased estimates of expected future interest rates.

Liquidity Preference Theory

Diminution of the risks associated with bond ownership is a feature of the unbiased expectations theory. While subject to variation, both money risk and credit risk generally are viewed as positively related to the maturity of a debt instrument. This suggests that owning long-term bonds is riskier that owning short-term bonds. Given this "constitutional weakness" on the long side, the liquidity preferences of risk-averse investors will influence their portfolio selections. They will prefer to own shorter term securities unless they are compensated for the additional risk associated with owning long-term bonds. Such considerations form the basis of the liquidity preference theory of the term structure of interest rates.[12]

If risk-averse bond traders are compensated for assuming risk, bond interest rates will contain a risk premium. Forward rates no longer are unbiased estimates of expected future interest rates. The bias in forward rates, as shown in 3.18, is in the amount of the risk (or liquidity) premium. That is, the forward rate exceeds the expected future interest rate by the amount of the liquidity premium ($_{t+i}L_j$). Alternatively, the forward rate is equal to the expected future interest rate plus the risk premium.

$$_{t+i}r_j - {}_{t+i}\rho_j = {}_{t+i}L_j, \tag{3.18}$$

where $_{t+i}L_j$ is the liquidity (or risk) premium on a j-year bond available i years from now.

The bias in forward rates varies with the maturity of a debt instrument. Generally, the longer the maturity of an instrument, the higher is the risk premium. This reflects the notion that both default risk and money risk normally increase with the maturity of a debt instrument. If risk and maturity are strictly positively related, then the term structure of liquidity premiums is upward sloping. That is the case in 3.19.

$$0 < {}_{t+1}L_1 < {}_{t+2}L_1 < {}_{t+3}L_1 < \cdots < {}_{t+n}L_1 \tag{3.19}$$

The presence of a term structure of liquidity premiums imparts an upward bias to the term structure of interest rates. If for, example, the expected interest rate is anticipated to remain the same, the yield curve is ascending. This case is depicted in Figure 3.10 below.

The yield curve will also be ascending if future interest rates are expected to increase. In the case where expected interest rates are expected to fall, the shape of yield curve can be ascending, horizontal, or descending. It depends on the pattern of term structure of expected interest rates in relation to the term structure of liquidity premiums.

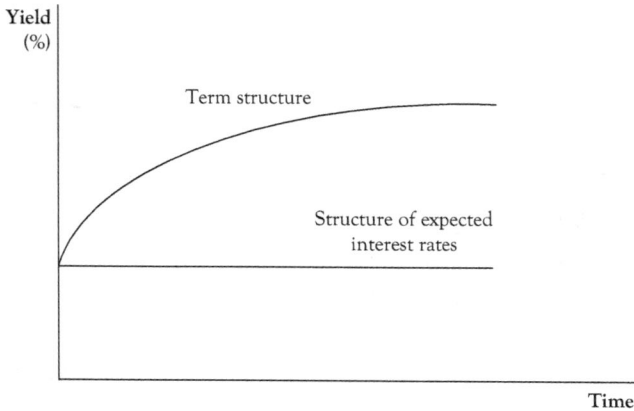

Figure 3.10 Term structure of interest rates.

In the case of the descending yield curve, for example, the positive slope of the term structure of liquidity premiums is not of sufficient magnitude to offset a downward sloping term structure of expected interest rates.

The upward bias in the term structure under the liquidity preference theory is consistent with historical patterns in rates. From an empirical perspective, the yield curve most often is ascending, and is frequently referred to as the normal yield curve. Empirical dominance of the normal yield curve is precisely what one would expect under the liquidity preference theory of the term structure.

Market Segmentation Theory

The final theory of the term structure is the market segmentation theory. Markets for bonds of different maturity are segmented, and bonds of different maturity do not serve as substitutes for one another. The rationale for such market segmentation is the risk-averse behavior of market participants. In this case, however, the primary concern is with income risk, rather than money or default risk.

Income risk is the risk that relevant future income flows are subject to wide variation. One strategy for attempting to reduce this type of risk exposure is through the careful selection of bond maturities. Maturity selection, in this case, assumes the form of definite maturity preferences on the part of both individual borrowers and lenders.

Borrowers may reduce income risk by matching the maturity of their debt issue with their anticipated future cash flows. A corporation borrowing to finance a new plant, for example, may prefer to issue a long-term bond so that repayments coincide with the cash flow generated with its expanded production capacity.

Lenders, too, may have very specific maturity preferences. Households face income risk when accumulating assets in order to finance college education for their offspring. In order to reduce that risk, they may select debt instruments whose maturities are temporally aligned with dates of those anticipated college education expenses.

Financial institutions interested in reducing their income risk frequently do so through maturity matching. That is, they may attempt to match the maturity structure of their assets with the maturity of their liabilities. Banks, with a preponderance of short- and intermediate-term liabilities, may accomplish this by selecting short and intermediate-term assets for their portfolios. If interest rates subsequently increase, both revenues and costs rise. With rate decreases, revenues and costs fall commensurately.

In contrast to banks, life insurance companies have liabilities that are long-term and somewhat predictable. Maturity matching, in their case, involves the selection of longer-term bonds. These may include corporate bonds and mortgages.

Under the strict version of the market segmentation theory, borrowers and lenders have very specific maturity preferences, and are disinclined to deviate from those preferences. Bonds of different maturity are not substitutable for one another, and the term structure is determined by the supply and demand for securities at each level of maturity. Changes in supply or demand conditions for a particular level of maturity, in turn, result in a shift in the term structure of interest rates.

A different debt management policy by the Treasury, for example, will have an impact on the yield curve. The decision to issue a larger portion of the debt in the form of long-term bonds will increase long-term rates relative to short-term rates. Accordingly, the slope of the yield curve increases. Similarly, more long-term corporate borrowing is expected to increase long-term rates without spilling over into short term maturities.

A more moderate version of the segmented markets theory also has the term structure determined by specific maturity preferences on the

part of both borrowers and lenders.[13] With somewhat less rigid preferences, market participants may be enticed to deviate from their "preferred
habitat" if the inducement is sufficient. If long-term rates rise significantly
relative to short-term rates, banks and other depository institutions may
choose to lengthen the maturity structure of their assets. This might occur
even though the maturity structure of their liabilities remains unchanged.
In the absence of sizable yield inducements, however, the expectation is
that market participants will adhere to their preferred maturities.

CHAPTER 4

Central Banks and the Money Supply

Banks, Bank Lending, and Money

Commercial banks are profit-oriented depository institutions. Bank customers place deposits with these institutions, and also use these bank deposits to make payments. That is, banks deposits are used as money. Since the bulk of the money supply resides in commercial banks, banks are often viewed as custodians of our money supply.

Commercial banks have an even larger monetary role because they are a conduit for the implementation of monetary policy. Currently, the most common way for the money supply to increase is through bank lending. When a bank makes a loan, the proceeds of the loan are in the form of an increase in the customer's deposit balance at the bank. Payment in this form is satisfactory to the bank customer because bank deposits are used as money. The customer can now spend this new deposit to purchase the item he/she is financing through credit.

The impact of the bank loan on the balance sheet of the bank is shown as transaction 1) in Exhibit 4.1. Bank A, the lending bank, has an additional loan in its portfolio (Loan +). The offsetting liability entry is the increased deposit balance of the borrowing customer (DD√ +).

When Bank A extends credit to a customer in this fashion, the money supply increases. That is because the proceeds of the loan is *new* deposit money. The aggregate money supply is now higher than it was before. Bank A now holds more deposit money. Every other bank in the system has the same amount of deposit money as before. Changes in the money supply are shown in equation 4.1.

$$M1 \, (\uparrow) = DD\surd \, (\uparrow) + C \qquad\qquad (4.1)$$

BANK A			
1)	Loan	+	DD√	+
2)	Reserves	−	DD√	−

Exhibit 4.1 Bank Loan

The reason that banks make loans to their customers is that it is profitable to do so. Assume that the interest rate on the loan made by Bank A is 5%. Assume, as well, that DD√ is a noninterest bearing deposit account. The spread on this loan is 5%. If the customer does not default on the loan, this is a profitable transaction for the bank.[1]

Given the profitability of such loans, the question is why the Bank A does not make a zillion loans. The answer is that Bank A's lending is constrained by the availability of its bank reserves. That is apparent once the customer borrowing from Bank A spends that newly-created money, e.g., the customer purchases a house. If the person selling the house banks at another bank, Bank B, money for the home purchase is now transferred (through the payments system) from Bank A to Bank B. Thus, while the newly-created money by Bank A is not lost to the banking system, it is lost to Bank A. Bank reserves follow the deposit money to Bank B when the check for the home purchase clears. That is, when Bank A repatriates (through the clearing system) the check for the home purchase, it gives reserves in exchange for the check. Transaction 2), in Exhibit 4.1 shows the loss of reserves at Bank B as well a reduced deposit liability. The latter occurs when the check for the house purchase is cancelled.

The results of combining transactions 1) and 2) appear in Exhibit 4.2. Bank A has an additional asset in the form of a bank loan. It acquired the asset through the loss of bank reserves. Thus, when a bank makes a loan, it can expect to lose reserves in the amount of the loan. It is the availability of bank reserves, then, that constrains the volume of lending undertaken by an individual bank.

Acquiring bank reserves is important to banks. An individual bank can increase its reserves in a number of ways. In competition with other

BANK A	
Loans +	
Reserves −	

Exhibit 4.2 Net Effects of a Bank Loan

banks, it can lure more customers. When they deposit, they bring reserves. A bank can also liquidate other assets that it holds in order to augment its reserves. Another potential source of bank reserves is through issuing liabilities, e.g., by borrowing reserves in the federal funds market.

Each of these cases is a zero-sum game. When one bank gains reserves, another bank in the system loses reserves. Net additions to bank reserves for all banks collectively most often originate through monetary policy. The model of the money supply presented in the next section allows for the investigation of both sources and uses of bank reserves. The techniques employed by central banks to increase the total quantity of bank reserves are integrated into the model.

A Model of the Money Supply

This money supply model is used to examine factors that determine the total quantity of money. In its basic form, the components are the level of base money (B), the base money multiplier (m), and the quantity of money (M). The model is presented in the form of both levels and differences (absolute changes).

$$M = B\,(m) \tag{4.2}$$

$$dM = dB\,(m) + B\,(dm) \tag{4.3}$$

Equation 4.2 states that the level of money (money supply) is equal to the level of base money (monetary base or high-powered money) times the level of the base money multiplier. Equation 4.3 expresses the same relationship in terms of differences. The change in the money supply (dM) depends on changes in the monetary base (dB) and changes in the money multiplier (dm). The M1 measure of money is used in this chapter, although it is possible to use the same general model for other measures.

Base Money

The monetary base is the primary form of money. It varies with the type of money used, and generally serves as the foundation for other elements of the money supply. In the case of commodity money, the levels of M and B are the same. Assume, for example, that gold coins are the only form of money. These gold coins serve as the monetary base. Base money is equal to the total quantity of gold coins (G), which is also the level of the money supply. With B and M the same number (equation 4.4), the money multiplier assumes the trivial value of one. Exhibit 4.3 shows the value of the money multiplier under different monetary systems.

$$G = B = M \qquad (4.4)$$

With fiduciary and fiat monies, the size of the money multiplier depends upon whether banks practice 100% reserve banking or fractional reserve banking. 100% reserve banking is when a banking institution holds bank reserves in the proportion of 100% of its deposit liabilities (Bank reserves are the cash holdings of a bank). With fractional reserve banking, a bank's cash reserves are less than 100% of its deposit liabilities.

Fiduciary money is a hybrid arrangement. It consists of an underlying commodity money, and fiduciary elements that are convertible into commodity money on demand. Assuming again that the commodity

Types of money	m
Commodity money	1
Fiduciary money	
100% reserve banking	1
Fractional reserve banking	>1
Fiat money	
100% reserve banking	1
Fractional reserve banking	>1

Exhibit 4.3 Values for m Under Different Monetary Systems

money is in the form of gold coins, the total quantity of these gold coins (G) is the monetary base. There are now alternative uses of the monetary base. A portion is used as circulating money (G_M); the remainder, as bank reserves (G_B). This partition appears in equation 4.5.

The total money supply (equation 4.6) is equal to the quantity of circulating gold coins (G_M) plus the quantity of circulating fiduciary money (FG_M) that is convertible into G_M. Fiduciary money is issued by banking institutions. With 100% reserve banking, $G_B = FG_M$. Consequently, $M = B$, and the size of the money multiplier is one. Banks are warehousing money.

$$B = G_M + G_B \qquad\qquad (4.5)$$

$$M = G_M + FG_M \qquad\qquad (4.6)$$

When banks enter the lending business, they practice fractional reserve banking. They either lend a portion of their reserves directly or, alternatively, make additional loans by issuing new fiduciary money. Bank reserves now equal only a portion of deposit liabilities, i.e., $G_B < FG_M$. FG_M includes both convertible currency and bank deposit money, which is only indirectly convertible. Individuals can convert bank deposits into convertible currency and, then, convert that currency into monetary gold. The important issue here is that the money multiplier is now greater than one ($m > 1$). Banks are no longer just storing money, but are affecting the size of the money stock.

As noted in Chapter 1, the adoption of fiat money was not a spontaneous market development. Governments confiscated (through forced exchanges) all monetary gold. In addition, laws were passed making it illegal to use gold as an exchange medium. Hence, both elements on the right-hand side of equations 4.5 and 4.6 were no longer available for monetary use, at least in their previous capacities.

The monetary system was reconstituted. The currency and bank deposits previously used as exchange media were still so employed. With no convertibility option (direct or indirect), however, these monies were now fiat money (FM). This is indicated in equation 4.8. Equation 4.7 is the new monetary base, which now consists of total bank reserves plus currency in circulation outside banks.

$$B = R + C \qquad (4.7)$$

$$M = FM = DD\sqrt{} + C, \qquad (4.8)$$

where R is total bank reserves,

C is currency in circulation outside banks,

FM is the total quantity of fiat money, and

$DD\sqrt{}$ is total checkable deposits.

It is possible to have 100% reserve banking with fiat money. In that case, $R = DD\sqrt{}$. In practice, fiat money invariably is coupled with fractional reserve banking. Consequently, the money multiplier for our current monetary system is greater that one.

The Base Money Equation

The base money equation is a relationship showing the total quantity of base money as well as the uses and sources of the base. This equation is an accounting identity, and is derived by combining the balance sheet for the central bank with the Treasury monetary account. In the United States, the combined balance sheet for all 12 Federal Reserve Banks is used as the central bank balance sheet. Exhibit 4.4 shows that balance sheet.

Assets		Liabilities	
(TS)	U.S. Treasury Securities	Federal Reserve Notes:	
(MTG)	Mortgage Securities	(FRN_P)	owned by the public
(D)	Discounts and Advances	(FRN_T)	owned by the Treasury
(CIPC)	Cash Items in the Process of collection	(FRN_B)	owned by commercial banks
(FE)	Foreign Exchange	Deposits:	
(GC)	Gold Certificates	(MBD)	owned by commercial banks
(SDRC)	Special Drawing Right Certificates	(TRD)	owned by the Treasury
(TC_{FRB})	Treasury Currency Held by Federal Reserve Banks	(FD)	owned by Foreign Central Banks and International Institutions
(OFRA)	Other Assets minus Other Liabilities and Capital Accounts	(DACI)	Deferred Availability of Cash Items

Exhibit 4.4 Combined Balance Sheet for Federal Reserve Banks

Equation 4.9 is the base money equation for the U.S.[2] Nearly all the entries are from the Federal Reserve balance sheet. Because base money is either used as bank reserves (R) or circulating currency (C), the sum of R and C is known as the uses of base money. Total bank reserves (R) are viewed as the Federal Reserve defines them: total commercial bank balances at Federal Reserve Banks (MBD) plus total bank vault cash (BVC). Bank vault cash consists of currency holdings by commercial banks. It is in the form of coins issued by the U.S. Treasury (TC_B) and paper notes issued by Federal Reserve banks (FRN_B).

$$4 \; B \equiv R + C \equiv TS + MTG + D + F + FE + G + SDR$$
$$+ TC + OFRA - TCH - TRD - FD \qquad (4.9)$$

Currency in circulation (C) is total currency circulating outside of banks. It consists of Treasury-issued coins owned by the public (TC_p) and Federal Reserve Notes owned by the public (FRN_p). When an individual goes to the bank (or a teller machine) and withdraws currency, the level of the monetary base remains unchanged but the uses of the monetary base have changed. C (in the form of FRNp) increases and R (FRN_B, a component of bank vault cash) falls. If an individual deposits currency, it, likewise, has no effect on the level of base money. The composition of base money, however, again changes.

All variables to the right of the identity sign (starting with TS) are sources of the monetary base. They include both factors of increase and factors of decrease. Those with a positive sign (TS, MTG, D, F, G,...) are factors of increase. If they increase (decrease), and the offsetting accounting entry in equation 4.9 is B, then the monetary base increases (decreases) on a one-to-one basis. Variables with a negative sign (TCH, TRD, FD) are factors of decrease. If they increase (decrease), and the offsetting accounting entry in the base money equation is B, the monetary base decreases (increases). The relationship is one-to-one, but inverse.

Federal Reserve Float (F)

The first four terms on the right-hand side of the base money equation (TS, MTG, D, and F) all originate in the Fed's balance sheet, and each is a factor of increase. Collectively (TS + MTG + D + F), they are called Federal Reserve Credit. This measures the quantity of base money that exists as a consequence of Federal Reserve actions. U.S. Treasury security holdings by Reserve Banks (TS), total mortgage securities owned by the Federal Reserve (MTG), and total commercial bank borrowings at the Federal Reserve Bank discount window (D) are the result of monetary policy and are discussed in the following sections.

The fourth, Federal Reserve float (F) is not due to monetary policy, but relates to the Federal Reserve procedures for clearing checks. It is calculated as the net of two items in the Federal Reserve balance sheet. Federal Reserve Float is equal to cash items in the process of collection (CIPC) minus deferred availability of cash items (DACI). That is, F = CIPC − DACI.

CIPC is a Federal Reserve asset, and records the volume of cash items in the form of checks that the Fed owns. Banks sent these checks to the Federal Reserve for clearing purposes. How the Federal Reserve pays for these checks is also recorded in the Fed's balance sheet. A few cash items receive immediate (or same day) credit, and the offsetting entry is a liability item in the Federal Reserve balance sheet: MBD. The bank submitting this cash item is credited with bank reserves in the form of a larger checking account balance at the Federal Reserve Bank.

While all banks eventually receive reserves (MBD) for checks they send to the Fed, they do not receive immediate reserve credit for most cash items. Instead, the Federal Reserve schedules to pay them reserves at a later date. According to the Fed's processing procedures, reserve payment will occur either one day or two days later. Timing of the payment is based on a predetermined geographic grid as well as the type of cash item submitted. That scheduled payment is entered in the balance sheet as liability item: deferred availability of cash items (DACI).

Note that the Federal Reserve's procedures for giving reserve credit to banks submitting cash items is not determined by when they collect on these checks. Consequently, their clearing procedures have monetary implications. The Federal Reserve often credits a bank (that sent a cash item) with reserves prior to collecting on the check. When that happens, total reserves in the banking system increase. Federal Reserve float is a measure of the total quantity of reserves in the banking system that entered in this manner. The volume of float varies from day-to-day and is influenced by factors such as weather conditions and the geographic features of market sales. Local purchases are less likely to result in Federal Reserve float than are national or international purchases.

An example of Federal Reserve float is shown in Exhibit 4.5. In transaction 1), Bank A sends a check to the Federal Reserve Bank. The offsetting entry in the bank's balance sheet is DACI (+), a scheduled payment of bank reserves by the Fed. In the Fed's balance sheet, both CIPC and DACI increase by the same amount. Hence, total Federal Reserve float is unchanged.

Assume that two days pass, and the Federal Reserve credits Bank A with reserves (MBD_A +) even though it has yet to collect on the check. This is transaction 2). If one combines transactions 1) and 2), the Federal Reserve balance sheet shows that CIPC is up, but DACI is not. Federal Reserve float increased with the second transaction.

The Fed will eventually collect on this check and when they do, they will reduce the reserves of the Bank B (MBD_B −), the bank upon which the check is drawn. This check will have effectively cleared the system, and there is no longer any float associated with that instrument. The increase in reserves at Bank A is exactly offset by a drop in reserves at Bank B. These entries are shown as transaction 3) in Exhibit 4.5.

Treasury Deposits (TRD)

Treasury deposits at Federal Reserve Banks (TRD) are also a variable in the base money equation. The U.S. Treasury uses Federal Reserve Banks

Federal Reserve Bank		Bank A	
1) CIPC +	1) DACI +	1) CHK −	
		1) DACI +	
	2) DACI −	2) DACI −	
	2) MBD_A +	2) MBD_A +	
3) CIPC −	3) MBD_B −		

	dF	=	dCIPC	−	dDACI
1)	0		+		+
2)	+		0		−
3)	−		−		0

Exhibit 4.5 Federal Reserve Float

for banking purposes. It owns deposit balances at Reserve banks, and writes checks on those balances in order to make payments. Those deposit balances are referred to as Treasury deposits (TRD), and appear as a liability item on the combined balance sheet for Federal Reserve Banks.

This item in the Fed's balance sheet (TRD) also appears as a factor of decrease in the base money equation 4.9. When the Treasury writes a check on its account, the check ultimately clears the banking system. The commercial bank submitting the check to the Federal Reserve receives deposit credit at a Federal Reserve Bank. Thus, bank reserves (and base money, B) increase, but TRD falls when the Federal Reserve Bank cancels the check the Treasury wrote to make the payment. The opposite happens when someone sends a check to the Treasury and the Treasury deposits that check at a Reserve Bank. TRD increases and MBD decreases.

Consider an example where individual A, who banks at Bank A, makes a tax payment to the Treasury. Payment by individual A is in the form of a check drawn on Bank A. The T-accounts for this transaction are in Exhibit 4.6. Only final entries in the T-accounts are shown, i.e., intermediate transactions such as the deposit and the clearing of the check do not appear.

Having written a check to pay his taxes, individual A now has a lower checking account balance (DD√ −). The offsetting balance sheet entry is a decline in his net worth (NW). That occurs because the tax payment is not a *quid pro quo* transaction. The tax payment is compulsory with no specific goods or services received in exchange.

The balance sheet for Bank A shows individual A's lower deposit balance. This is offset by Bank A's lower deposit balance at the Federal Reserve Bank (MBD −). The Treasury deposited individual A's check at the Federal Reserve Bank. When the Fed sent that check back to Bank A (for clearing purposes), it lowered Bank A's deposit balance as payment for the check.

Individual A		Bank A	
DD√ −	NW −	MBD −	DD√ −

Federal Reserve Bank		Treasury	
	TRD +	TRD +	NW +
	MBD −		

Exhibit 4.6 Individual Tax Payment to the Treasury

The Treasury now has a larger cash balance at the Federal Reserve Bank (TRD +), with the offsetting entry an increase in its new worth (NW +). With its higher cash balances, the Treasury is now in a position to purchase more goods and services. As a consequence of paying taxes, the private sector (individual A) is in a position to purchase fewer.

From a monetary standpoint, base money is lower. That is because TRD is a factor of decrease in the base money equation. The reduction in base money appears in T-accounts as a decline in MBD. These deposits are a component of bank reserves. Thus, in equation 4.9, B (in the form of R) is lower, while TRD is higher.

Treasury management of its cash position, then, affects the quantity of base money. Hence, Treasury actions can potentially impair the effectiveness of monetary policy. For that reason, there is daily communication between the Treasury and the Federal Reserve concerning Treasury budgetary activity for that day. This allows the central bank an opportunity to take actions that offset the monetary repercussions of Treasury fiscal actions.

The (Base) Money Multiplier

In a world of fiat money with fractional reserve banking, the money multiplier is greater than one. This means that whenever the level of base money changes, the money supply changes by some multiple of that change in the base. The extent of the change in money supply depends on the size of the base money multipler (m). The M1-multiplier is presented as equation 4.10. There are three factors that determine the size of m: k, r_r, and r_e.[3]

$$m = (1 + k)/(r_r + r_e + k) \qquad (4.10)$$

where k is the currency ratio,

r_r is the average reserve ratio requirement, and

r_e is the excess reserve ratio.

$$k = C/DD\sqrt{} \qquad (4.11)$$

where C is total currency in circulation outside banks, and $DD\sqrt{}$ is total checkable deposits.

$$r_r = RR/DD\sqrt{} \qquad (4.12)$$

where RR is total required reserves for banking institutions.

$$r_e = ER/DD\sqrt{} \qquad (4.13)$$

where ER is total excess reserves held by banks.

The Currency Ratio: k

The currency ratio (equation 4.11) is a behavioral ratio, whose value is determined by the general public. It measures how much currency the public chooses to hold relative to their holdings of checkable deposits. k is also an aggregate ratio, i.e., the value of k is an average ratio for the entire public.

Because k appears in both the numerator and denominator of the money multiplier, it is not immediately clear whether the relationship between m and k is direct or inverse. If k increases, both the numerator and denominator of m increase. Similarly, a decline in k results in a lower value for both the numerator and denominator.

While the mathematics is not developed here, for reasonable values for the other parameters in m, the relationship between m and k is inverse ($\partial m / \partial k < 0$.) The change in m divided by the change in k is less than zero. Increases in the currency ratio cause the money multiplier to fall; decreases cause it to rise.

The reason for this inverse relationship becomes apparent by examining equations 4.14 and 4.15. It has to do with how the monetary base is used. Every unit of base money that is held as circulating currency (C) maps into exactly one unit of money (M1). The relationship is one-to-one. On the other hand, every unit of base money that is used as bank reserves (R) maps to some multiple of that value in terms of deposit money (DD$\sqrt{}$). That relationship is one-to-x, where x > 1.

$$B = R + C \qquad (4.14)$$

$$M1 = DD\sqrt{} + C \qquad (4.15)$$

Thus, base money supports a larger money supply when it is used as bank reserves. The reason is fractional reserve banking (R < DD$\sqrt{}$). When individuals deposit their currency in banks, that currency becomes bank reserves (R ↑ and C ↓). These bank reserves support some multiple level of deposit money in a world of fractional reserve banking. Had the individuals continued using the currency instead of depositing it, there would be no such multiple impact on the money supply.

When the currency ratio (k) changes so too, does the base money multiplier (m). Consequently the portfolio behavior of the general public has monetary significance. Decisions concerning how much currency to hold relative to deposit money influence the level of the money supply through changes in the money multiplier.

There are seasonal, cyclical, and secular influences on the public's portfolio behavior (and, thus, k). An important seasonal influence is the Christmas holiday season in the United States. Related to the sharp acceleration in December retail sales is a greater demand for currency to effectuate those sales. The higher currency ratio has a depressive influence on the money multiplier and the money stock. That upward blip in the currency-ratio generally is reversed in January, when retail sales most often fall.

One of the more dramatic movements in the currency-ratio occurred during the Great Depression in the 1930s. The public lost confidence in commercial banks and many chose to hold their money in the form of currency rather than bank deposits. This led to a sharp decline in the money multiplier, which contributed significantly to a massive decline in the money supply.

Another factor affecting the currency ratio is the process of economic development. The ratio tends to fall with economic growth as financial institutions and markets develop. The public typically reduces its reliance on currency, and more frequently makes payment with deposit money. One hundred years ago, it was not uncommon for U.S. workers to receive their wages in the form of currency. That rarely occurs today. Most individuals receive payment either by check or via direct deposit.

The Reserve Ratio Requirement: r_r

Banking is a very highly regulated industry. That is true even in those countries where most markets are open, and voluntary exchange generally is permitted. One form of banking regulation is reserve requirements.

This regulation requires banks to hold reserves in a specified minimum ratio to their deposit liabilities.

While it is possible to have reserve requirements for several categories of bank deposits, only the reserve requirement on checkable deposits (r_r) is considered here. If r_r = 10%, for example, banks are required to hold reserves in the proportion of at least 10% of their checkable deposit liabilities. Equation 4.16 shows the calculation for required reserves (RR). If r_r = 10%, and total DD√ is equal to one million dollars, RR = $100,000.

$$RR = r_r \, DD\sqrt{} \qquad (4.16)$$

The reserve ratio requirement is in the denominator of the money multiplier. This indicates an inverse relationship between r_r and m. A higher reserve ratio requirement means a lower money multiplier. A lower money multiplier, in turn, results in a lower money supply. A lower reserve ratio requirement, by contrast, leads to monetary expansion.

The inverse relationship between r_r and m exists because reserve requirements restrict the amount of lending (and money creation) banks can potentially undertake. However, recent changes in the reserve ratio requirements for U.S. banks indicate that, for this country, r_r is less of a constraint on bank lending than it was in the past. These changes in U.S. reserve requirements, and their implications for the U.S. money multiplier, are described in Section C.

Excess Reserve Ratio: r_e

Reserve requirements specify legal minimum proportions of reserves to deposits. Banks are free to hold additional reserves, and often have. These additional reserves are called excess reserves. In equation 4.17, the volume of excess reserves (ER) is calculated as the difference between total reserves (R) and required reserves (RR).

$$ER = R - RR \qquad (4.17)$$

Excess reserves are low-earning assets and holding them generally reduces bank profits.[4] Hence, banks must have an overriding motive if they are to hold any excess reserves. When they do so, it is generally because of uncertainties surrounding the management of their cash position. These problems relate to difficulties associated with forecasting deposit withdrawals and loan demand.

Banks do not know, with certainty, the amount of deposit withdrawals and loan demand that will occur on any given day. Both of these activities result in a reduction of a bank's reserve position. Consequently, banks must have a strategy for coping with these uncertainties. One such strategy is called asset management. This involves holding liquid assets in the bank portfolio. When pressures on the cash position do occur, these liquid assets can be sold. Because excess reserves are the most liquid of assets, they sometimes are held for this purpose.

When banks hold excess reserves, those reserves are not available to support bank lending activity. From the perspective of bank lending (and the accompanying money creation), it is as if the reserves do not exist. That is, the holding of excess reserves reduces the potential size of the money supply.

It does so through the money multiplier. The excess reserve ratio (r_e) is in the denominator of the multiplier, indicating an inverse relationship. As banks hold more excess reserves, in relation to their checkable deposits $(r_e \uparrow)$, the money multiplier is smaller. A smaller value for m implies a reduction in M1. Reducing excess reserve holdings (relative to DD$\sqrt{}$), on the other hand, expands the money supply.

A Numeric Example

The general public, commercial banks, and the government potentially influence the size of the money stock through the money multiplier, whose value depends on the levels of k, r_r, and r_e. k is determined by the behavior of the general public; r_e, by the behavior of commercial banks. Given the practice of bank sweeps in the United States (pp. 85–87), r_r is also largely determined by commercial banks. That is the case even though stated reserve requirements originate through government.

Other things equal, all three are in an inverse relation to m. Assume, for example, that k = .5, r_r = .05, and r_e = .05.

$$m = (1 + k)/(r_r + r_e + k) = (1.5)/(0.6) = 2.5 \qquad (4.18)$$

From equation 4.2, a multiplier of 2.5 indicates that the money supply is 2.5 times the level of the monetary base. Moreover, from equation 4.3, any change in the level of the monetary base results in a change in the money supply that is 2.5 times the change in the quantity of base money. This multiplier effect, which is the direct consequence of fractional reserve banking, has very important consequences for monetary policy. If bank reserves are increased through monetary policy, there will be a multiple expansion of bank deposits. A reduction in reserves leads to a multiple contraction of bank deposits. This phenomenon is known as the multiple expansion and contraction of bank credit.

General Instruments of Monetary Control

There are four general instruments of monetary policy: 1) open market operations; 2) discount window/discount rate; 3) reserve ratio requirements; and 4) interest payments on bank reserves. They are called general instruments because their effects are widespread. That is, their usage has an impact throughout the country, and across most markets. This has important political implications, especially for democracies. In situations where monetary policy inflicts economic hardship, it is more politically palatable (or considered a "fair game") if it affects nearly everyone.

Open Market Operations

History

Open market operations are the purchase and sale of securities by the central bank. They are by far the most important monetary-policy instrument in the United States today. This was not always the case. Indeed, when the Federal Reserve Act was passed in 1913, there was no understanding of this instrument. The Act did empower individual Reserve banks to purchase U.S. government securities and bankers acceptances. The motives were twofold: 1) to allow Reserve Banks to earn additional income to cover operating expenses; and, 2) to promote international trade.

The potential impact of such purchases (and sales) on economic activity was discovered by accident in the early 1920s. This discovery led to the formation of a series of committees within the Federal Reserve System. The motive was to coordinate security purchases and sales by individual banks. If open market purchases and sales did significantly affect the economy, an attempt to coordinate these actions made sense.

Ultimately, open market purchases and sales were codified into law with the Banking Acts of 1933 and 1935. The 1933 legislation provided for a Federal Open Market Committee (FOMC) that would assume responsibility for the conduct of open market operations. No longer were individual Banks allowed to purchase and sell securities. Instead, purchases and sales were done on behalf of all 12 Federal Reserve Banks. Individual Banks could refrain from participation, but that option was removed in the Banking Act of 1935.

The Process

Open market operations originate with the FOMC, which meets approximately every six weeks. Intra-meeting decisions occasionally occur via conference call, but they are the exception. FOMC meetings include both the presentation of economic forecasts and policy discussion. They end with the issuance of a set of instructions (called a directive) to the Account Manager of the Federal Reserve Bank of New York. The directive is written in general terms, but the Account Manager is in attendance at the meetings to capture the intent of the FOMC committee. The Account Manager then uses the directive to carry out open market operations on behalf of all twelve Reserve Banks.

Federal Reserve purchases and sales of securities occur via a process known as the "go around." Once the Account Manager decides a course of action, he/she informs traders at the New York Federal Reserve Bank. These traders, in turn, contact security dealer firms in the New York City money market. Actual trades are between the New York Fed and these dealer firms.

Assume, for example, that the Account Manager's decision is to buy a given quantity of U.S. government securities within a specific maturity range. Traders contact individuals at the security dealer firms and ask them if they have any such securities for sale. If they do, traders want to know how many and at what price? Dealer firms offering securities are asked if they are willing to hold firm on their offers for the next 30 minutes. All offers are posted at the New York Fed, and the decision is made to accept or reject the offers. Typically, the Fed buys securities with the lowest offer price (and the highest yield). Once the decision is made, traders again contact the security firms and inform them if their offers are accepted or rejected.

Most U.S. open market operations involve secondary-market purchases or sales of U.S. government securities. Even though U.S. Treasury securities are exchanged, the U.S. Treasury (who issued the securities) is not involved. The Treasury issued these securities at some time in the past, and someone else owns them now.

The fact that open market operations are conducted in the secondary market for U.S. government securities has an important implication. They do not affect the overall size of U.S. government debt. What changes is the composition of ownership of U.S. Treasury debt. If the Fed purchases securities, more of the debt is now owned by Federal Reserve Banks, and less is owned by security dealer firms.

Accounting for Open Market Operations

The monetary impact of open market operations is determined by how the transactions are financed. Purchases and sales by the Federal Reserve are paid with *bank reserves*. Payment is made on a pass-through basis, and involves the Fed, a set of security dealer firms, and the clearing banks for the dealer firms.

The T-accounts associated with an open market purchase are presented in Exhibit 4.7. As a simplification, it is assumed that only one security dealer firm (Firm D) and one clearing bank (Bank D) are involved. The combined balance sheet for Federal Reserve Banks shows an increase in

Federal Reserve Bank			Bank D			Firm D	
TS	+	MBD	+	MBD	+	DD√	+	DD√	+
							TS	−

Exhibit 4.7 T-Accounts for Open Market Purchase

Treasury securities (TS) on the asset side. This records the acquisition of securities.

The offsetting entry is an increase in MBD on the right-hand (liability) side. MBD is total commercial bank deposits at Federal Reserve Banks. The increase in this item on the Fed's balance sheet indicates how the Federal Reserve paid for securities acquired in the open market purchase. The Fed does not directly pay the security dealer firm (Firm D) but, instead, pays the clearing bank (Bank D) for the security dealer firm. It does so by increasing that bank's deposit balance at the Fed. Bank D then passes the payment through to dealer firm.

The pass-through payment is shown on the T-account for Bank D. This clearing bank now has a larger deposit balance at the Federal Reserve Bank, but also has an increase in its deposit liabilities (DD√). This increased checking account balance is owned by the security dealer firm (Firm D), and represents the pass-through payment from the clearing bank to Firm D. The T-account for Firm D now shows both the increase in its deposit balance at Bank D and a reduction in its holdings of U.S. government securities.

Open Market Operations and the Money Supply

Commercial bank balances at Reserve Banks (or member bank deposits, MBD) count as bank reserves. When the Federal Reserve pays for securities by increasing these balances, the total volume of reserves in the banking system increases. Because banks need reserves in order to make loans, banks are now in a position to extend more credit.

This has important implications for the money supply. When banks make additional loans, the money supply increases. Indeed, in a world of fractional reserve banking, there will be a multiple expansion of bank credit. In the above example, the raw material for such a multiple expansion of bank deposit money appears in the form of additional bank reserves at Bank D.

The world of fiat money is a world of inflation, and this secular decline in the purchasing power of money largely is the consequence of government expansion of the money supply. For many market-oriented economies in the industrial world, expansion the money supply occurs mainly through such open market purchases. In these economies, open market operations now serve as the "printing press."

Open market purchases (and sales) of securities affect the base money equation 4.9. Federal Reserve purchases increase TS (a factor of increase), with the offsetting entry an increase in base money (B). In the basic money supply model (4.2), the increase in B results in an increase in M1. The multiple expansion of deposit money occurs through the workings of the money multiplier, which is larger than one in a world of fiat money and fractional reserve banking. The impact of those changes on equation 4.2) is shown below.

$$M1 \ (\uparrow) = B(\uparrow)m \tag{4.19}$$

Transmission of Bank Reserves

In this country, new reserves brought into the system via open market purchases are initially located in New York City banks. That is because open market operations are with dealer firms and clearing banks in New York City. Some of the new reserves may be used to support lending activity in this locale. However, reserves tend to follow economic activity and the newly created reserves can be used to support lending activity in any part of the country. Avenues for the transfer of these reserves from Bank D to other parts of the country (or world) are many. Only a few are mentioned here.

One possibility is that a New York City firm borrows money from Bank D and spends the proceeds of the loan outside the city. Another is that a firm outside New York City borrows from Bank D and, likewise, spends the funds outside of New York City. Still another possibility is that the reserves will leave New York City through activity in the federal funds market. This last possibility is examined in more detail.

The federal funds market is one where immediately available (or same day) funds are loaned. These funds must be immediately available because many of the loans are for one day only. This market has long been a medium for the transfer of bank reserves. Activity in the market commenced in the early 1920s, with banks loaning reserves to one another on an overnight basis. The market flourished during the final third of 20th

Bank D		Federal Reserve Bank		Bank DBQ			
MBD_D −		MBD_D −		MBD_{DBQ} +	FFP +		
FFS +		MBD_{DBO} +					

Exhibit 4.8 Federal Funds Market Transaction

century, with many small banks joining the ranks of large banks by using the market as a medium for adjusting their short-term reserve positions. Some of the more aggressive larger banks commenced to use the market for more than simply adjusting their reserve position. The reserves they acquire are employed to support their long-term loan portfolios.

Exhibit 4.8 shows T-accounts for a typical federal-funds market transaction. In this example, Bank D loans reserves to Bank DBQ in Dubuque, Iowa. Bank D instructs the Federal Reserve to transfer a portion of its reserves to the account of Bank DBQ. When this happens, there is no change in the aggregate volume of commercial bank balances at Federal Reserve Banks. However, there is a change in the ownership composition of these balances. The Fed's balance sheet shows an increase in MBD_{DBQ} (Bank DBQ's balance) and a decrease MBD_D (Bank D's balance).

Bank D has swapped assets. Its balance sheet shows an increase in federal funds sold (FFS +) and a decrease in its reserve balance at the Fed (MBD_D −). The balance sheet for Bank DBQ reflects its larger reserve balance at the Fed (MBD_{DBQ} +), and an increased liability for federal funds purchased (FFP +). The bank reserves created by the New York Federal Reserve Bank's open market purchase now reside with Bank DBQ in Dubuque, Iowa.

Discount Rate/Discount Window

A second general instrument of monetary policy is the discount rate. This is the interest rate the Federal Reserve Bank charges banking institutions when they borrow reserves at the discount window. When the Federal Reserve System was initially organized in 1914, the country was still operating with fiduciary money (the gold standard). At that time, the discount rate was the principal instrument of monetary control. The United States was following in the footsteps of the United Kingdom, where the bank rate of Bank of England had long been the centerpiece of monetary policy. But, there was more to it than that. Open market operations were not understood in 1914, and reserve ratio requirements were set by statute. Hence, the discount rate was the *only* general instrument of monetary control.

Individual Reserve Banks set the discount rate with the approval of the Federal Reserve Board. There were many instances, early in the history of the Federal Reserve System, when the discount rate was not uniform across all Federal Reserve Districts. That is uncommon today, where a uniform discount rate policy across Federal Reserve Districts reflects the high degree of integration of financial markets in the United States.

For decades, the Federal Reserve employed nonprice rationing in managing the discount window. This was due, in part, to prolonged periods where the discount rate was set below the federal funds rate. To limit bank borrowing through the discount window, the Fed established rules and guidelines for appropriate commercial bank use of the discount window. These rules and regulations were known as the Federal Reserve's "administration" of the discount window. The Fed made it known that banks should use the discount window mainly as a means of managing their short-term reserve position. Continuous borrowing was frowned upon and considered a violation of Fed policy.

The Federal Reserve recently changed its discount window policy. Regulation A was revised in a manner that eliminated much of the nonprice rationing at the discount window. The Fed increased the discount rate by 150 basis points, and placed it 100 basis points above the federal funds rate. All banks in sound condition, and with adequate collateral, now are permitted discount-window borrowing at their own discretion. With the discount rate above the federal funds rate, banks generally have an incentive to adjust their reserve positions in the federal funds market.[5]

During the first two decades of the Federal Reserve System, the discount window was a major source of bank reserves and of variation in the monetary base. The proportion of reserves coming through the discount window did not fall below 37% in the 1920s, and was in excess of 80% in 1921. During this period, changes in the discount rate were of major significance. That is no longer the case. With the ascendance of open market operations as the primary instrument of policy, the importance of the discount window has steadily diminished.

In recent decades, the ratio of borrowings at the discount window to total bank reserves was often is less than 1%. This indicates that virtually none of the bank reserves were coming through the discount window. Although this is an overstatement, current changes in the discount rate are tantamount to a price change in a market where there is no activity.

While the significance of the discount rate has diminished, officials of the Federal Reserve are not ready to abolish the discount window. It can play a major role when the Fed assumes the posture of lender of last resort. The central bank plays that role in situations that could result in financial panic. Three recent incidents were the stock market crash in 1987, the terrorist attacks on the New York City Twin Towers in 2001, and during the Great Recession of 2008–2009. During such episodes, the Federal Reserve often is desirous of making sizable volumes of bank reserves available on short notice. The discount window is well suited for this purpose.

Both open market purchases and lending through the discount window provide additional reserves to the banking system. From a policy perspective, however, they differ in one critical respect. In the case of open market purchases, the Federal Reserve takes the initiative. For loans through the discount window, individual commercial banks must initiate activity. That is, nothing happens until a bank approaches the Fed and requests a loan.

T-Accounts for a discount window loan appear in Exhibit 4.9. Bank A requests and receives a loan from a Federal Reserve Bank. The loan appears in the Fed's balance sheet as an increase in D (Discounts and Advances). The proceeds of the loan are made available to Bank A in the form of an increased deposit balance at the Federal Reserve Bank. Hence, MBD_A increases on the right-hand side of the Fed's balance sheet.

Bank A owns that deposit balance, which shows as a left-hand side entry in its balance sheet (MBD_A +). The offsetting entry is on the liability

Federal Reserve Bank			Bank A		
D	+	MBD_A +	MBD_A +	D	+

Exhibit 4.9 Discount Window Loan

side (D +). This additional liability reflects Bank A's obligation to repay that loan at a later date.

Discounts and Advances (D), from the Fed's balance sheet, are a factor of increase in the Base Money Equation 4.9. Hence, a discount-window loan increases the level of monetary base. Repayment of the loan has the opposite effect. It decreases the monetary base. The affect that increased lending through the discount window has on the money supply is seen in equation 4.20 below. Again, with fractional reserve banking, an increase in base money results in a multiple expansion of deposit money.

$$M1 (\uparrow) = (B \uparrow) \cdot m \qquad (4.20)$$

Reserve Ratio Requirements

Banking started as individual proprietorships or partnerships that were unregulated. Today, most banks are corporations that are very heavily regulated by government. Reserve requirements are one form of government regulation. These regulations specify that commercial banks must hold reserves in some minimum proportion to bank deposit liabilities.

When the Federal Reserve Act was passed in 1913, reserve requirements were set by statute. The Banking Act of 1935 gave the Federal Reserve Board the authority to set (and change) reserve requirements for all federally chartered banks. The Depository Institution Deregulation and Monetary Control Act of 1980 extended the Federal Reserve's authority to cover all depository institutions—both bank and nonbank institutions, and state chartered as well as federally chartered depository institutions.

Unlike open market operations and lending through the discount window, changes in reserve requirements do not affect the total volume of reserves in the banking system. Instead, changes in reserve requirements affect the maximum amount of deposits a given volume of reserves will support. When reserve requirements are increased, available bank reserves potentially support a smaller quantity of bank deposits. A decrease in reserve requirements has the opposite effect. Available reserves can now support a larger quantity of bank deposits.

Bank A in Exhibit 4.10 below has $100,000 in deposits. With a 10% reserve requirement, its required reserves are $10,000. Because Bank A

Bank A			
Reserves	$10,000	DD√	$100,000

Exhibit 4.10 Balance Sheet – Bank A

has exactly that amount of reserves, it is holding zero excess reserves. In banking parlance, the bank is "loaned out."

If the central bank lowers the reserve requirement to 5%, the total quantity of reserves in the banking system is not affected. That is true for Bank A as well, which still has $10,000 in reserves. However, its required reserves have fallen to $5,000. With excess reserves in the amount of $5,000, it is now in a position to make additional loans. Doing so will expand the total quantity of deposit money.

Were the central bank to, instead, increase the reserve requirement, the opposite occurs. While Bank A's reserves remain the same, it now has a deficient reserve position, or negative excess reserves. It must now make fewer loans which contracts the total quantity of deposit money.[6]

Such changes in reserve requirements have their monetary impact through the money multiplier. As discussed in pages 73–74, the reserve requirement is in the denominator of the money multiplier. Hence, the size of the multiplier moves inversely with the level of the reserve requirement. For example, a reduction in the reserve requirement increases the size of the multiplier, as in equation 4.21 below.

$$M1 \ (\uparrow) = B \cdot m \ (\uparrow) \tag{4.21}$$

Changes in reserve requirements have been infrequently used as a means of adjusting monetary policy. For that reason, they have been a minor instrument of monetary policy. Recently, many banks in the United States commenced new banking practices (with sanction from the Federal Reserve) that further diminished the significance of reserve requirements.

Beginning in 1994, these commercial banks began to reclassify a portion of their checkable deposits liabilities as money market deposit accounts (MMDAs). Such reclassifications, referred to as sweeps, were motivated by the desire to limit the impact of reserve ratio requirements.[7] Because they were done only for reserve accounting purposes, sweeps did not alter the nature of the securities owned by bank customers. However, banks employing sweeps now had two sets of books (or balance sheets). One set was for reserve accounting; the other, for general dissemination.

Use of sweeps effectively lowered a bank's reserve requirements. The reason is that checkable deposits were subject to reserve requirements, while MMDAs were not.[8] By reducing the bank's level of checkable deposits (for reserve accounting purposes), sweeps had the effect of reducing a bank's required reserve holdings. The same level of checkable deposits now called for fewer required reserves. Banks using these sweeps had, in effect, lowered their own required reserve ratio. The bank's new required reserve ratio was below the one specified by the Federal Reserve.

Following is a summary of the critical features of these new reserve ratio requirements:

- For banks using sweeps, the reserve requirement ratio is not the one stated by the Federal Reserve. It is below the Federal Reserve's reserve ratio requirement.
- Because required reserves are calculated from a different set of bank liabilities than those reported to the public, the new reserve requirement is not visible to the general public.
- The reserve requirement is determined by individual banks, although it is conditioned by the Federal Reserve's official reserve requirement.
- The reserve requirement varies by bank, and can differ for banks with identical liability structures (but different sweeps).
- Changes in reserve requirements set by the Federal Reserve may elicit little response from the banking system.

Given the implications for monetary policy, the last feature requires elaboration. Following sweeps, the new lower reserve requirement is not a binding constraint for many banks. The reserves they choose to hold to meet customer demands for credit, and for potential adverse check clearings, are above the level of required reserves. For banks in such a position, an increase or decrease in the Federal Reserve's reserve requirements is likely to leave them in a similar position. That is, their required reserves are still below those they choose to hold for normal banking operations. As a consequence, the change in the Fed's reserve requirements may have no impact on the bank's level of desired reserve holdings and lending policies.

With reserve requirements for many banks below those specified by the Fed, and with the Federal Reserve's reserve requirements having only a negligible impact on many banks, an alternative version of the base money multiplier is presented. In contrast to the multiplier in equation 4.10, it focuses attention on total reserve holdings of banks instead of partitioning them into required and excess reserves.

Let $r = r_r + r_e$, where r is an aggregate reserve ratio for banks. Given the Federal Reserve's diminished role in establishing reserve requirements, r is largely determined by commercial bank behavior. With the currency ratio (k) determined by the behavior of the general public, the size of the reconstituted money multiplier (equation 4.22) is largely determined by the behavior of economic agents in the private sector.

$$m = (1 + k)/(r + k) \qquad (4.22)$$

Interest on Bank Reserves

In 2008, the Federal Reserve began paying interest on commercial bank deposits at Federal Reserve Banks (MBD). Prior to this time the Federal Reserve paid no interest on these deposits. Because MBD are a component of the cash position of a commercial bank, this change in Federal Reserve policy increases the income banks earn by holding this form of cash.

Payment of interest on MBD (i_{MBD}) also gives the Federal Reserve a new policy instrument. By varying the interest paid on these deposits, the Federal Reserve can influence the desired level of excess reserve holdings by commercial banks. Because excess reserves are reserves not employed to support bank lending, changes in the level of excess reserve holdings by banks influences both the volume of bank lending and the level of the money supply.

An increase in i_{MBD} increases commercial bank returns on excess reserves. They now have an incentive to make fewer loans and to hold more excess reserves. If they do so, the money supply decreases. A reduction in i_{MBD} has the opposite effect. It reduces the incentive for banks to hold excess reserves. If banks respond by making additional loans, the money supply increases.

Thus, Federal Reserve changes in i_{MBD} have their impact on the money supply through the base money multiplier. The aggregate excess reserve ratio for commercial banks (r_e) is now a function of the rate the Fed pays on deposits that banks hold at Federal Reserve banks, or i_{MBD}. The revised version of the multiplier is shown in equation 4.23. A higher level of i_{MBD} increases r_e and reduces the level of base money multiplier; a lower level of i_{MBD} does the opposite. It lowers r_e and increases the money multiplier.

$$m = (1 + k)/[r_r + r_e(i_{MBD}) + k] \qquad (4.23)$$

Selective Credit Controls

When a central bank directs credit to specific markets, specific firms, or specific regions of the country, this is known as selective credit controls. This practice is common in socialist countries and/or less developed countries where governments often desire greater control over how resources are employed in the economy. In a socialist country, for example, the government may want to increase the size of the manufacturing sector of the economy. If the central bank channels more credit to this sector of the economy, it can increase the prospects for greater economic activity in manufacturing.

In the U.S. recession of 2008–2009, the Federal Reserve deviated from it historical pattern of relying on general instruments of monetary control. Instead, it moved into the realm of selective credit controls. It did so through the direct placement of bank reserves, both in specific banks and in a specific sector of the U.S. economy.

Purchase of Bank Equity (BKEQ)

The Federal Reserve coerced the largest U.S. banks to sell bank equity to the Fed. The motive was to increase the capital position of those banks. The Federal Reserve was concerned about the capital adequacy of these banks once they wrote down the value of their assets to reflect the reduced quality of their loan portfolios.

Some interpreted this as an attempt by the U.S. government to social-ize banks in the country. This partly reflected the unprecedented nature of this action. But, it also reflected a legitimate concern. At issue was whether the government would eventually become a major shareholder in these banks. If that were to occur, banks would be effectively socialized. Moreover, the government would be in a position to engage in selective credit controls on a continuing basis.

The immediate consequence of the Fed's actions was to increase the capital position of the banks involved. It did so by directly placing bank reserves in those banks in exchange for bank equity. The impact on bal-ance sheets is shown in Exhibit 4.11. The Federal Reserve now holds bank equity (BKEQ +) on the asset side of its balance sheet. This purchase of commercial bank stock was financed by increasing its liabilities in the form of a larger deposit balance for the bank selling equity to the Fed.

This new deposit balance (MBD +) is an asset for the selling bank, Bank A, and appears on the left-hand side of its balance sheet. The offset-ting entry for Bank A is an increase in bank equity (BKEQ +). The higher level of Bank A's equity represents an increase in the capital position of the bank. A similar increase bank capital occurs for each bank selling its equity to the Federal Reserve.

While the Federal Reserve's motivation was to increase bank capi-tal for individual banks, these actions also have monetary implications. Because the Fed paid for its new bank equity holdings with bank reserves, base money increases. In the equation for base money, 4.9, BKEQ is a component of Other Federal Reserve Accounts (OFRA). When this factor of increase rises so too, does the monetary base. With additional reserves (MBD +), banks are now in a position to make more loans and create additional deposit money.

Federal Reserve Banks		Bank A	
BKEQ +	MBD +	MBD +	BKEQ +

Exhibit 4.11 Federal Reserve Purchase of Bank Equity

Purchase of Mortgage Securities (MTG)

The Federal Reserve also engaged in selective credit controls when it directly placed reserves with individual commercial banks in exchange for mortgage securities during the Great Recession of 2008–2009. Through such exchanges, the Fed was directly channeling credit to a specific sector of the U.S. economy—the housing sector. The motive was to provide financial support for that sector which was at the epicenter of the very pronounced decline in economic activity.

When the Federal Reserve purchased mortgage securities from banks, it not only provided direct support to the housing sector, but also support for individual commercial banks. The mortgages sold by these banks were often "nonperforming," i.e., the borrower was in arrears on equity payments, interest payments, or both. Selling these toxic assets to the Federal Reserve enabled many of these banks to avoid severe financial stress and, for some, the prospect of bankruptcy. From the perspective of the Federal Reserve, shoring up individual bank balance sheets in this manner reduced the possibility of contagion, where the failure of one bank can lead to the failure of many banks, and possibly resulting in a general financial panic.

The impact of Federal Reserve purchases of toxic mortgage securities from individual commercial banks is shown in Exhibit 4.12. The Federal Reserve now owns mortgage securities which it financed by crediting the account of the selling bank, Bank A, with a deposit at the Federal Reserve Bank. Bank A shows that new deposit balance as an asset (MBD +) on the left-hand side of its balance sheet. The offsetting entry is a drop in its holdings of mortgage securities (MTG –).

The Federal Reserve's payment for these securities was in the form of new bank reserves. In the base money equation 4.9, MTG increases as does B. The banking system, in general, is now in a position to extend

Federal Reserve Banks		Bank A	
MTG +	MBD +	MBD +	
		MTG –	

Exhibit 4.12 Federal Reserve Purchase of Mortgage Securities

additional credit. The Federal Reserve provided a massive amount of bank reserves to the financial system in this manner during and after the recession of 2008–2009. From a position of zero holdings prior to 2008, MTG became one of the larger assets in the Federal Reserve's portfolio.

BKEQ and MTG are both on the asset side of the combined balance sheet for Federal Reserve Banks, and are factors of increase in the base money equation. Hence, both the purchase of bank equity and the purchase of mortgage securities by the Federal Reserve increase the quantity of base money and, potentially, the money supply. Those changes are summarized in equation 4.24. The sale of these securities has the opposite effect. It decreases the quantity of base money and the money supply.

$$M (\uparrow) = B (\uparrow) \cdot m \qquad\qquad (4.24)$$

Closed Market Operations

From a global perspective, most money creation is not based on the policy instruments discussed above. The largest share of the world's fiat money is created in less developed countries and/or countries that have embraced socialism.

Open market operations are often not an option for these countries because financial markets are so poorly developed.[9] Poorly developed markets, however, have not hampered their ability to create fiat money. Money supply increases in these countries are often the result of a process referred to here as closed market operations.

Monetary policy generally is driven by government financing operations. Governments wish to spend more money than the Treasury obtains in tax revenues. With no active market for Treasury securities, the government cannot finance additional spending by selling Treasury bonds in the open market. Instead, the Treasury issues new bonds and places them directly with the central bank. The central bank pays for these securities by crediting the deposit account of the Treasury at the central bank. The Treasury now is in a position to spend more.

The T-accounts for this closed market operation are in Exhibit 4.13. The Treasury balance sheet shows an increase in its cash balance at the central bank (TRD +). The increase in Treasury liabilities (TS +) represents

Treasury			Central Bank		
TRD	+	TS	+	TS	+	TRD	+

Exhibit 4.13 Closed Market Operations

the bonds (or Treasury Securities) placed directly with the central bank. The balance sheet for the central bank shows that this institution now owns more Treasury securities (TS +). The offsetting entry is the increase in the Treasury's deposit balance (TRD +) with the central bank.

Once the Treasury spends these new cash balances, Treasury deposits at the central bank (TRD) are transformed into bank reserves (MBD). Banks are now in a position to extend additional credit. Massive amounts of fiat money are created in this fashion.

APPENDIX A

Derivation of the Base Money Equation

The base money equation is an accounting identity. It is derived from two other identities: 1) the balance sheet for the central bank; and 2), the Treasury Monetary Account. These identities summarize the monetary influences of the central bank and the Treasury respectively.

The derivation here is for the U.S. monetary system. Variables in the base money equation reflecting Federal Reserve policy are from the combined balance sheet for all 12 Federal Reserve Banks. Exhibit 4.14 presents that balance sheet. Equation 4.25 shows the identity between total Federal Reserve assets and the summation of total liabilities and capital accounts for Federal Reserve Banks.

$$TS + MTG + D + CIPC + FE + GC + SDRC + TC_{FRB} + OFRA$$
$$\equiv FRN_P + FRN_T + FRN_B + MBD + TRD + FD + DACI \qquad (4.25)$$

U.S. Treasury activities influence the quantity of base money in several ways. It issues that portion of circulating currency (Treasury currency, or TC) which is in the form of coins. The Treasury also holds the

Assets	Liabilities
(TS) U.S. Treasury Securities (MTG) Mortgage Securities (D) Discounts and Advances (CIPC) Cash Items in the Process of collection (FE) Foreign Exchange (GC) Gold Certificates (SDRC) Special Drawing Right Certificates (TC_{FRB}) Treasury Currency Held by Federal Reserve Banks (OFRA) Other Assets minus Other Liabilities and Capital Accounts	Federal Reserve Notes: (FRN_P) owned by the public (FRN_T) owned by the Treasury (FRN_B) owned by commercial banks Deposits: (MBD) owned by commercial banks (TRD) owned by the Treasury (FD) owned by Foreign Central Banks and International Institutions (DACI) Deferred Availability of Cash Items

Exhibit 4.14 Combined Balance Sheet for Federal Reserve Banks

vast quantities of gold (G) owned by the U.S. government. It is also the repository for Special Drawing Rights (SDRs) owned by the U.S. government. SDRs are a form of bookkeeping money issued by the International Monetary Fund to individual countries. They are used exclusively to settle payments imbalances between countries.

Gold and SDRs holdings of the U.S. government have monetary significance when the Treasury monetizes them. It does this by issuing claims on these assets to the Federal Reserve Banks. Gold certificates (GC) are claims on the government's gold holdings; Special Drawing Rights Certificates (SDRC), claims on the government's SDR balances. In exchange for these ownership claims issued to the Federal Reserve, the Treasury receives an increase in its cash balance at Federal Reserve Banks (TRD). When such an exchange occurs, Gold and/or SDRs have been monetized. Once the Treasury spends these new cash balances, bank reserves (R) and bank deposit money (DD√) increase.

The Treasury Monetary Account (4.26) captures the impact of these Treasury operations on the money supply. It is assumed that 100% of the gold and SDR holdings of the Treasury are monetized. It follows that G = GC and SDR = SDRC. Currency (or coins) issued by the Treasury (TC) are partitioned into those by owned by banks, the general public, and Federal Reserve Banks, respectively.

$$G + SDR + TC \equiv GC + SDRC + TC_B + TC_P + TC_{FRB} \qquad (4.26)$$

where, G = gold holdings of the Treasury

SDR = Special Drawing Rights held by the Treasury

GC = Gold Certificates owned by the Federal Reserve

$SDRC$ = Special Drawing Right Certificates owned by the Federal Reserve

TC = Treasury Currency issued

TC_B = Treasury Currency owned by banks

TC_P = Treasury Currency owned by the general public, and

TC_{FRB} = Treasury Currency owned by Federal Reserve Banks.

The base money equation is obtained by aggregating equations 4.25 and 4.26 and, then, solving for base money. Initially, the left-hand side of both equations is summed and is equated to the summation of the right-hand side of these equations.

$$TS + MTG + D + CIPC + FE + GC + SDRC + TC_{FRB} + OFRA + G +$$
$$SDR + TC \equiv FRN_P + FRN_T + FRN_B + MBD + TRD + FD + DACI +$$
$$GC + SDRC + TC_B + TC_P + TC_{FRB} \qquad (4.27)$$

Several substitutions are made to simplify this identity. Federal Reserve float (F) is defined as CIPC – DACI, and entered on the left-hand side. TCH (Treasury Cash Holdings) is substituted for FRN_T. GC, SDRC, and TC_{FRB} appear on both sides of the identity. Consequently, they cancel. The result is identity 4.28.

$$TS + MTG + D + F + FE + G + SDR + TC + OFRA \equiv FRN_P + TCH$$
$$+ FRN_B + MBD + TRD + FD + TC_B + TC_P \qquad (4.28)$$

The remaining task is to solve for base money (B), which is equal to $R + C$. Employing the Federal Reserve's definition, bank reserves (R) are equal to total bank vault cash (or, $TC_B + FRN_B$) plus aggregate commercial bank balances at Federal Reserve Banks (MBD). Currency in circulation outside banks (C) is equal to $TC_P + FRN_P$. Hence, $B = TC_B + FRN_B + MBD + TC_P + FRN_P$. Collecting these terms and transposing the others yields the base money equation.

$$B = TS + MTG + D + F + FE + G + SDR + TC + OFRA$$
$$- TCH - TRD - FD \qquad (4.29)$$

APPENDIX B

Derivation of the Base Money Multiplier

The basic money supply model (equation 4.30) relates the level of the monetary base to the level of the money supply. Connecting the two is the base money multiplier. The money multiplier (m) is the number which, when multiplied times the level of base money (B), yields the money supply (M). In a world of fiat money with fractional reserve banking, the value of the money multiplier is greater than one. The size of the multiplier varies with the measure of money under consideration. The multiplier derived here is for the M1 measure of money.

Several assumptions are employed. First, a multibank system is assumed. Second, the reserve ratio requirement (r_r) is contemporaneous and fixed. It applies only to checkable deposits ($DD\sqrt{}$). Finally, the excess reserve (r_e) ratio and the currency ratio (k) also are fixed. All three of these ratios, which were discussed on pages 72–75, are presented as equations 4.31–4.33.

$$M = B \cdot m \qquad (4.30)$$

$$r_r = RR/DD\sqrt{} \qquad (4.31)$$

$$r_e = ER/DD\sqrt{} \qquad (4.32)$$

$$k = C/DD\sqrt{} \qquad (4.33)$$

where RR is aggregate required reserves,

ER is aggregate excess reserves, and

C is total currency in circulation outside banks.

As indicated in 4.34, base money (B) is measured as summation of total bank reserves (R) and total currency in circulation outside of banks (C). Total bank reserves, in turn, are partitioned into required reserves and excess reserves.

$$B = R + C = RR + ER + C \tag{4.34}$$

From equations 4.31–4.33, the following substitutions are made: r_r (DD√) is substituted for RR; r_e(DD√) for ER; and, k(DD√) for C.

$$B = r_r(DD\surd) + r_e(DD\surd) + k(DD\surd) \tag{4.35}$$

$$= (r_r + r_e + k)DD\surd$$

Solving 4.35 for DD√ yields 4.36. This expression for DD√ is substituted into 4.37, an equation for the M1 measure of money. The result is 4.38, the basic money supply model for M1-money. The term in brackets is the money supply multiplier (m).

$$DD\surd = B/(r_r + r_e + k) \tag{4.36}$$

$$M1 = DD\surd + C = DD\surd + k(DD\surd) = (1 + k)DD\surd \tag{4.37}$$

$$M1 = B\,[(1 + k)/r_r + r_e + k] \tag{4.38}$$

Given recent changes impacting on reserve ratio requirements in this country, an alternative version of the money multiplier is also included. It is the multiplier in 4.22 above. This multiplier uses an aggregate reserve ratio (r) for banks. That is, let $r = r_r + r_e$. Substitution of r into 4.38 yields this second money multiplier.

$$m = (1 + k)/(r + k) \tag{4.39}$$

CHAPTER 5

Monetary Policy

Monetary Policy in a World of Fiat Money

Most of man's accumulated experience is with commodity money. Fiduciary money, by contrast, is relatively new. It has only been with us for the last several centuries. Like commodity money, the origin of fiduciary money generally is viewed as a spontaneous market development. The supposition is that the process that led to both of these types of money involved attempts by individual economic agents to reduce the transactions costs associated with voluntary exchange.

Nearly all money in use today is fiat money. As largely a 20th century phenomenon, this is a relatively new form of money. Unlike the other two types of money, the adoption of fiat money was not a spontaneous market development. It mainly came about through coercive acts of governments. Those undertaken by the U.S. government in 1933 are a case in point. President Roosevelt, acting on authority granted by Congress, issued an executive order making it illegal to hold monetary gold, with all outstanding monetary gold confiscated through forced exchanges.[1] These actions effectively eliminated the convertibility option of the existing fiduciary money arrangement. Contracts relating to money ownership were not the only ones affected. All other contracts (such as bonds) written in terms of monetary gold were, likewise, summarily voided.

While individual economic agents generally preferred fiduciary money to fiat money, governments clearly did not.[2] The convertibility option associated with fiduciary money significantly constrained government control over money. The reason was that excessive issue of fiduciary money threatened the integrity of the convertibility option, raising the specter of a financial panic. Elimination of the convertibility option removed that constraint, and gave individual governments the freedom to issue money at will.

With less than a century of continuous usage of fiat money, our relative lack of experience gives us a limited window for assessing the consequences of government control of money. One thing about fiat money, however, is abundantly clear. Under government control, changes in the quantity of money are not a random process. Decisions by governments across the world have led to unprecedented increases in the quantity of money.

Effects of Fiat Money

Despite our limited experience with fiat money, enough time has passed to permit a few tentative generalizations relating to its usage.

Monetary Nationalism

The adoption of fiat money accomplished its major objective. Governments now have much greater control over money. Instead of a global monetary system integrated by the use of a common money (or monies), we now have monetary nationalism. With a few exceptions, each country has its own money. Each of these monies is loosely linked to one another by activities in foreign exchange markets. Under this arrangement, individual countries are free to employ that particular monetary policy that best suits policymakers in the country. This was a major motive for moving away from fiduciary money. In this respect, then, the adoption of fiat money was a success.

Inflation

While national governments have much greater monetary autonomy in a world of fiat money, virtually all of them have used their monetary sovereignty in a similar manner. They have increased the quantity of fiat money. As a consequence, all countries share a common experience: inflation. The inflation has been continuous and, in many cases, pronounced. As a result, the period since the adoption of fiat money has appropriately been dubbed the age of inflation.

Data assembled by economic historians suggest that this title is well deserved. Rates of inflation that followed the adoption of fiat money are

Table 5.1 Four Great Inflations in England (Average Annual
Inflation Rate)

I. Medieval Inflation (1265–1360)	0.6
II. 16th Century Inflation (1475–1650)	1.3
III. 18th Century Inflation (1730–1810)	1.3
IV. 20th Century Fiat Money Inflation (1931–2007)	5.6

Sources: Phelps Brown and Hopkins (1956). Data for 1954–2007 are from *International Financial Statistics: Yearbook*, (various issues, International Monetary Fund).

without precedent. David H. Fischer identifies four great inflations of the past millennium: the medieval inflation, the 16th century inflation, the 18th century inflation, and the 20th century inflation.[3] Each of these inflations was widespread as evidenced by its impact on residents in many different countries. Inflation data for one of those countries, England, are presented in Table 5.1. Note that the rate of price increase during the inflation of the 20th century far exceeds that for any of the other three great inflations. Average annual fiat money inflation in England, 5.6%, was more than four times the average inflation rate for the 16th and 18th century inflations, and nearly 10 times the average inflation rate recorded during the great medieval inflation.

The preeminence of the 20th century inflation, in terms of magnitude, is even more remarkable when one considers that fiat money was only widely adopted about one-third of the way through the century. As a consequence, most of the 20th century inflation accrued in the last half of the century. Average annual inflation in the United Kingdom, for example, was 6.5% from 1960–2002. Numerous other countries experienced double-digit average inflation for this period. This data leaves little doubt that the other three great inflations pale by comparison with 20th century inflation.

The effects of 20th century fiat money inflation on the purchasing power of money have been devastating. Table 5.2 shows the cumulative decline in the purchasing power of money in each of 55 countries for the 47 year period from 1960–2007. Note the breadth of the inflation experience. Massive depreciation in the exchange value of money occurred in all 55 countries. None fared better than Panama, where money lost more

Table 5.2 Percent Depreciation in Value of Money: 1960–2007

Panama	70.3	Angola	99+
Germany	74.7	Argentina	99+
Japan	81.4	Bolivia	99+
United States	85.7	Brazil	99+
Canada	86.1	Chile	99+
France	89.2	Colombia	99+
Morocco	90.2	Costa Rica	99+
Norway	90.2	Ecuador	99+
Sweden	90.2	Ghana	99+
Australia	91.2	Israel	99+
Denmark	91.2	Mexico	99+
Finland	91.6	Nicaragua	99+
Cameroon (62)	93.3	Nigeria	99+
United Kingdom	93.9	Paraguay	99+
Ireland	95.0	Peru	99+
Italy	95.7	Poland (70)	99+
India	96.6	Romania (70)	99+
Rwanda (66)	97.0	Russia (92)	99+
Spain	97.0	Sudan	99+
Burundi (64)	97.8	Tanzania (65)	99+
Swaziland (65)	97.7	Turkey	99+
South Africa	97.9	Uganda (81)	99+
El Salvador	97.9	Uruguay	99+
Egypt	98.2	Venezuela	99+
Korea	98.3	Zaire/Rep. Congo (63)	99+
Philippines	98.6	Zimbabwe (65)	99+
Portugal	98.6		
Greece	98.8		
Kenya	98.9		

Note: Data series for some countries begin after 1960. Starting dates for those countries are indicated by parentheses, e.g., Zimbabwe (65).

Source: International Financial Statistics: Yearbook (various issues, International Monetary Fund).

than 70% of its value. The median country on the list is Greece, where the exchange value of money declined by 98.8%. In 26 of the countries, money lost in excess of 99% of its purchasing power.

Reduced Services of Money

The plummeting exchange value of the world's currencies has important implications for the services provided by money. Throughout the world, money has largely ceased to serve as a long-run store of value. This is manifested differently in various parts of the world. In the United States, individuals hold money balances almost exclusively for transactions purposes. Wealth accumulation occurs primarily via other assets such as stocks, bonds, and real assets.

In the less developed countries, on the other hand, one frequently observes a plethora of partially completed homes. The decision to build a home in stages, and over a period of years, is grounded in economic logic. Given the depreciation in the purchasing power of money in those countries, the poor of the world would never achieve home ownership through savings accumulated in the form of money balances.

In the more extreme cases of inflation, money often is rejected as a medium of exchange. The transactions costs associated with using the country's money are deemed excessive. In rejecting the money of their own country, individuals sometimes select that of another country (such as U.S. dollars) for use as an exchange medium. This phenomenon is known as currency substitution. An alternative to currency substitution is reversion to barter. Even though the transactions costs associated with barter are often relatively high, in these cases, they are lower than when using money.

In responding to the monetary chaos they have created, governments often call in the old currency and replace it with a new currency. The rate of exchange can involve thousands of units of the old currency for one unit of the new. Because the old currency is discredited in a major way, it is common to give the new currency new colors and a new name. Once implemented, such monetary reform positions government to once again expand the quantity of fiat money at its own discretion.

Lower Economic Growth

Fiat money has been a vehicle for the transfer of massive quantities of resources from the private sector of the economy to government. This is especially true in many less developed countries, where money growth rates are relatively high. Historically, unpopular means such as taxation or other coercive measures have been the principal method for governments to increase their ownership of resources. The ability to print fiat money has given them an attractive alternative. By spending the money that they create, governments are able to wrest resources away from individuals without having recourse to more direct forms of coercion.

This additional source of finance has permitted 20th century governments to become much larger. A major consequence of the adoption of fiat money, then, is that it greatly enhanced the economic power of government relative to that of individuals. Given that more rapid economic growth generally is associated with greater individual economic freedom and more secure property rights, widespread use of fiat money has, no doubt, led to a reduction in world economic growth (relative to what it otherwise would have been). Because the alternative is a path not taken, it is difficult to know the magnitude of the reduction in living standards.

Expansion of Fiat Money: Motives

Our current age of inflation is a direct result of adopting fiat money. With inflation largely orchestrated by governments, the question of motivation arises. Is it in the self-interest of governments to expand the quantity of fiat money? The answer to this question is in the affirmative. Self-interested governments are driven by two principal motives.

One is seigniorage, or government revenue from money creation. Government control of money has permitted a significant reallocation of resources—from the private sector of the economy to government. Consequently, the world of fiat money is not only a world of inflation, but also one characterized by the rapid growth of government.

The second motive is found mainly among governments in several of the relatively industrial and market-oriented economies of the world. Influenced by the writings of British economist John Maynard Keynes, these governments have used monetary policy as a tool in the attempt to control movements in the aggregate economy. These efforts have resulted in significant money creation accompanied by inflation.

Seigniorge

The motive for most increases in the world money supply is seigniorage. Governments around the world consume vast quantities of resources. One way for them to wrest these resources from the private sector is taxation. As noted above, however, taxation generally is politically unpopular. Moreover, many governments of the world do not have fiscal systems in place that generate the quantity of tax revenues necessary to finance their desired expenditure programs. This is especially true in less developed countries, where greater use of currency in effectuating exchanges, more limited voluntary tax compliance, and the lack of legitimacy significantly hamper government's quest for tax revenues.

An alternative to taxation is for government to finance expenditures by printing money. This can assume several forms. First, government can simply print new currency and spend it. There are numerous historical examples of this. One occurred during the Revolutionary War in this country, when the Continental Congress authorized the printing of currency (Continentals) to pay soldiers and to finance other wartime expenditures.

A second form is where the Treasury issues new bonds and places them directly with the central bank. In return, the Treasury receives an increase in its cash balance at the central bank. When the Treasury spends this additional cash balance, the quantity of money in circulation rises. This form of money creation is described as closed market operations in Chapter 4. It is popular throughout much of the world, and accounts for the bulk of fiat money creation.

A third, and more subtle form, is when the central bank monetizes debt issued by the Treasury. This is mainly possible in countries (such as the United States) that have encouraged the development of open financial markets. Monetizing debt occurs when the Treasury finances its expenditures by issuing bonds in the market. Those purchasing the newly issued bonds lose cash balances. The central bank replenishes this loss of private-sector cash balances through an open market purchase (equivalent in value to the Treasury bond sales). This joint Treasury/central bank venture results in additional Treasury cash balances at the central bank with no (net) loss of cash balances in the private sector. When the Treasury spends its new cash balances, the money supply increases.

The Seigniorage Tax

Printing money is posed as an alternative to taxation. It too, however, is a form of taxation. Unlike other taxes, though, it is a hidden or covert tax. The burden of this tax is borne by holders of (real) money balances. They are not presented with a tax bill but, instead, find that the additional inflation occasioned by government money creation adversely affects their money holdings. These cash balances now purchase fewer goods and services than they did before, i.e., their real cash balances have decreased.

The nominal seigniorage (S), in this case, is the money value of the goods and services that government is able to buy with the money it prints. Assuming that all money is government money, nominal seigniorage is equal to the increase in the money supply (dM, where dM > 0). Equation 5.1 shows the level of nominal seigniorage.

$$S = dM \qquad (5.1)$$

$$s = dM/P = (dM/M) \ (M/P) \qquad (5.2)$$

The quantity of goods and services (dM/P) the government can actually purchase with this new money is the real seigniorage, or s. In equation 5.2, real seigniorage is written as the product of the rate of growth of the money supply (dM/M) and the quantity of real money balances (M/P). This permits us to see more clearly the genesis of real seigniorage.

The total seigniorage tax on holders of real money balances is equal to the growth rate of money (dM/M) times the level of real money balances (M/P). To demonstrate this, recall Fisher's quantity theory of money. A given growth rate for money increases the growth rate of prices by the same proportion. A 10% rate of money growth, for example, causes dP/P to be 10% higher than it otherwise would have been. Thus, real money balances depreciate by 10% more than they otherwise would, or by dM/M.

In equation 5.2, then, the growth rate of money is the tax rate that is applied to the quantity of real money balances, the tax base. The product of the two is the amount that real money balances fall as a consequence of money creation. This tax on holders of real money balances is precisely equal to the (real) government revenue from money creation, or s.

Maximum Seigniorage

The maximum amount of seigniorage government can collect is complicated by the fact that taxpayers are sensitive to tax rates. In this case, rational economic agents reduce their desired holdings of real money balances as inflation increases. That is, as the tax rate increases, the tax base declines. In equation 5.2, increases the growth rate of money (dM/M $\uparrow$) result in lower holdings of real money balances (M/P $\downarrow$).

Whether additional money creation increases real seigniorage depends on the relative strength of these two opposing forces. The tax rate elasticity of the tax base is the appropriate measure of this.

$$\eta = d(M/P)/(M/P)/d(dM/M)/(dM/M) \qquad (5.3)$$

Table 5.3 shows the various possibilities. If $\eta > -1$, the numerator is smaller (in absolute terms) than the denominator. Hence, the tax base is changing less rapidly than the tax rate. In this case, increases in the growth rate of money result in higher real seigniorage.

If (in absolute terms) the tax base changes more, in proportionate terms, than does the tax rate, $\eta < -1$. This is the third case in Table 5.3. The increased sensitivity of taxpayers to tax rates means that a higher

Table 5.3 Money Growth and Seigniorage

	dM/M	s
$\eta > -1$	$\uparrow$	$\uparrow$
$\eta = -1$	$\uparrow$	$\rightarrow$
$\eta < -1$	$\uparrow$	$\downarrow$

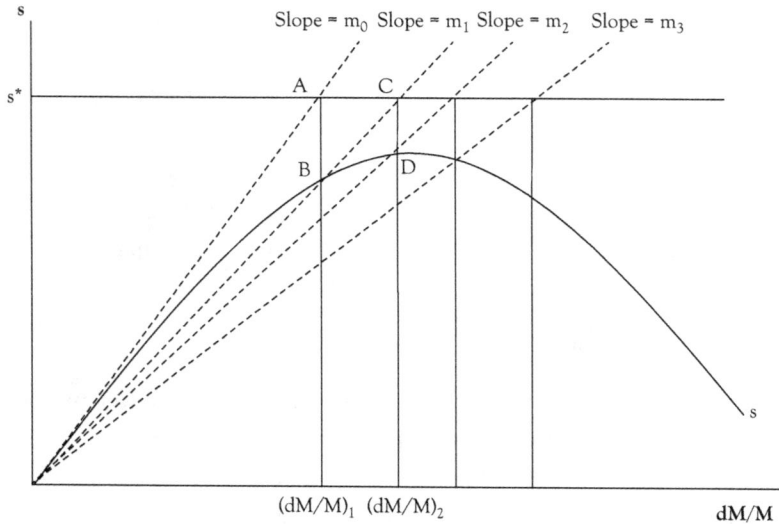

Figure 5.1 Seigniorage with hyperinflation

growth rate for money now results in less real seigniorage. A government desirous of more seigniorage must now reduce the growth rate of money.

It follows that a government interested in maximizing real seigniorage should increase the growth rate of money up to the point where $\eta = -1$. At this point, the (proportionate) increase in the tax rate is exactly offset by the (proportionate) decline in the tax base. Further increases in the growth rate of money reduce real seigniorage. In Figure 5.1, maximum seigniorage occurs with tax rate $(dM/M)_2$.

Hyperinflation

Inflation can degenerate into hyperinflation, or a very high rate of inflation. When this happens, inflation can reach hundreds or even thousands of percent per month. There have been numerous instances of hyperinflation, and all are associated with the use of fiat money. Without the constraint imposed by a convertibility option, governments are free to create massive quantities of money. Some have chosen to do so.

Data from some of the major 20th century episodes of hyperinflation are presented in Table 5.4. One of the most dramatic cases occurred in

Table 5.4 *Episodes of Hyperinflation*

Country	Dates	Average inflation rate (per month)
Germany	Aug. 1992–Nov. 1923	322
Greece	Nov. 1943–Nov. 1944	365
Hungary	Aug. 1945–July 1946	19,800
Poland	Jan. 1923–Jan. 1924	81
Russia	Dec. 1921–Jan. 1924	57

Source: Cagan, Philip (1956).

Hungary immediately after World War II. Inflation averaged 19,800% per month for nearly one year. To grasp the magnitude of this inflation, consider the impact on the price of a candy bar selling for $1. With this inflation rate, the price would increase to nearly 400 million dollars in two months.

Hyperinflation occurs when a government's quest for seigniorage becomes dynamically unstable. Government prints more money in order to spend more. But, the ensuing inflation means that government is actually able to purchase fewer goods and services than before. Therefore, the government prints even more money. This results in even higher inflation, again reducing the purchasing power of the money created by government. Additional money is created, and the acceleration of money growth eventually spirals out of control.

The massive quantities of money created by government put enormous upward pressure on the right-hand side of Fisher's equation of exchange. Huge increases in M are dissipated in the form of a rapid rise in P. But, a second factor is exacerbating the impact on P. The rapid increase in prices constitutes a sharp increase in the tax on holders of real money balances. Owners of money respond rationally by reducing their cash holdings. These reduced money holdings are manifested in the following way. People experiencing hyperinflation spend money nearly as quickly as they receive it. The result is very rapid increase in the velocity of circulation of money.

$$M V = P y \qquad (5.4)$$
$$\uparrow \uparrow \quad \ \ \uparrow$$

Hence, not only are rapid increases in M causing prices to soar, but increases in velocity are pushing prices even higher. With M and V both exerting upward pressure on P, P increases more than M. That is, real money balances are falling. While that is the intent of the general public (as owners of money balances), it creates a problem for governments. Government is creating money because of its purchasing power. By increasing velocity, the behavior of the general public is destroying that purchasing power.

At the epicenter of this dialectic is a level of desired real seigniorage that is inconsistent with the public's preferred holdings of real money balances. While government controls the nominal quantity of money, it does not control the quantity of real money balances. The latter is the result of portfolio decisions made by the general public.

A graphical version of this dialectic appears in Figure 5.1. Each point on the seigniorage curve (s) associates a level of real seigniorage with a given growth rate for money.[4] As is indicated in equation 5.2, what relates these two variables is the level of real money balances held by the public. Real seigniorage (s) is equal to the product of the growth rate of money and the level of real money balances. Money supply growth is the government-controlled tax rate, while the level of real cash balances is the tax base determined by the general public. For any given growth rate for money, there exists a *desired* level of real money balances for the general public. The product of the two yields the real seigniorage accruing to government when the general public is holding its desired real money balances. The seigniorage curve in Figure 5.1 is a locus of such points.

For a fixed level of actual real money balances (as opposed to a desired level), the graph of equation 5.2 becomes a linear relation with actual real money balances serving as the slope. Each level of money supply growth is proportionate to an associated level of real seigniorage. Several such linear rays are shown in Figure 5.1. Each corresponds to a different fixed level for real money balances. The declining slopes ($m_0 > m_1 > m_2 > m_3$) signify falling real money balances.

Each point where a linear ray intersects the seigniorage curve (e.g., B and D) is an equilibrium point. The public's desired holdings of real money balances (embedded in s) are equal to actual real money balances reflected in the slope of the linear ray. For all other points, disequilibrium obtains. In those instances, actual real money balances differ from desired holdings.

Assume that the government's desired real seigniorage is s*. The initial level of actual real money balances is m_0. The government increases the money supply growth to $(dM/M)_1$ in order to generate s* (at point A). At point A, however, the inflation rate occasioned by that money growth rate causes owners of real money balances to collectively reduce their holdings of real cash balances to the desired level (m_1) associated with that tax rate.[5] Real seigniorage falls to point B.

To reach its desired seigniorage, government now accelerates money growth to $(dM/M)_2$. In Figure 5.1, the movement is along the ray (with slope m_1) from point B to point C. The higher inflation rate associated with $(dM/M)_2$ again causes owners of real money balances to reduce their holdings, this time to m_2. The higher inflation and reduced money holdings again thwart government. Real seigniorage falls to point D. Again the government responds. Note that each time government accelerates money growth, real money balances are reduced, with ultimate result of hyperinflation.

Macroeconomic Management

For several of the world's relatively industrial and market-oriented countries, seigniorage is not the principal motive for government increases in the quantity of fiat money. Instead, governments have increased the money supply in an effort to achieve macroeconomic objectives such as increased economic growth, more moderate economic fluctuations, and reduced unemployment.[6]

Monetary policy employed for this purpose is called discretionary monetary policy, because central banks in these countries change the policy at their own discretion. Such discretion was very limited under fiduciary money arrangements, but has blossomed with the adoption of fiat money. Indeed, the abandonment of the gold standard in the 20th century was largely motivated by the desire of governments to have greater flexibility in the management of monetary policy.

The objectives of governments employing discretionary policy have varied. Some viewed discretionary monetary policy as a means to stimulate higher economic growth, although this goal is seldom mentioned today. On the other hand, virtually all governments now state long-term price stability as a major policy goal. A primary objective for devotees of discretionary monetary policies remains, however, the attempt to moderate short-term business cycle fluctuations.

This emphasis on short-term business fluctuations is more suitable to modern governments, where bureaucrats often possess short-term time horizons. It dates back to the confluence of three related events in the 1930s that provided the impetus for governments to more actively engage in discretionary economic policies. Those events were the Great Depression, the abandonment of the gold standard, and the influence of the writings of British economist John Maynard Keynes.

Keynes argued that moderating fluctuations would contribute in a significant way to improving material living standards. Moreover, he was confident that a judicious employment of government economic policies could accomplish this. On the monetary side, appropriate doses of monetary simulation and restriction where required. Stimulation was necessary when the economy lagged; monetary restriction, when an economy became overheated.

While use of monetary policy for this purpose is symmetrical in theory, it has not been in practice. Government policies have been heavily biased toward monetary stimulation. The result has been significant monetary expansion accompanied by secular inflation.

Discretionary Monetary Policy

Discretionary monetary policy is most feasible in countries such as the United States, where financial markets are both relatively open and more highly developed. Central banks in these countries adjust policy instruments in response to perceived changes in the economic environment. Often those changes in policy instruments are directed toward influencing target variables that, in turn, affect ultimate policy objectives such as aggregate output or the price level. Such procedures require knowledge of the monetary policy transmission mechanism, which specifies linkages between the policy instruments, policy targets, and the objectives of monetary policy. In the United States, the Federal Reserve's operational transmission mechanism relies upon interest rate targets.

Transmission Mechanisms

Knowledge of the transmission mechanism is essential for implementing activist monetary policies. This mechanism indicates, usually in a sequential fashion, how changes in the instruments of monetary policy actually bring about changes in economic activity. Views of economists differ concerning the nature of these linkages. Behind their disagreements are different theories of this monetary process. While an extensive discussion of alternative transmission mechanisms is not undertaken, two of the more conventional ones are presented. They are outlined in Exhibit 5.1.

Monetary policy is initiated through the use of policy instruments. The instrument variable in both of these transmission mechanisms is open market operations (OMO).

These operations are undertaken to affect the level of an immediate target. The immediate target, in turn, affects the level of the intermediate target which influences the ultimate objective (or objectives) of monetary policy. The objective variable for both transmission mechanisms is nominal income (Py), which can be decomposed into its component parts. They are the price level (P) and real output (y).

What differentiates the two transmission mechanisms are the targets employed. One uses an interest rate target; the other, a monetary aggregate target. The first transmission mechanism (Model I) employs an interest rate target. Use of interest rate targets has a long tradition among central banks. The bank rate has long been the centerpiece of monetary policy in England. Since its inception in 1913, Federal Reserve Banks in

Model	Instrument variable	Immediate target	Intermediate target	Policy objective
I	OMO →→→→→→→	i_{st} →→→→→→	r_{lt} →→→	P·y (P or y)
II	OMO →→→→→→→	B →→→→→→	M →→→→→	P·y (P or y)

Exhibit 5.1 Transmission Mechanisms

the United States have, for the most part, employed interest rate targets. Such targets have found favor with central banks in other countries, too.

This historical predilection by central banks for interest-rate targeting received 20th century theoretical support from Keynesian economists. Economists in this tradition argued that monetary policy primarily affects aggregate spending through its impact on interest rates. Given that such a perspective readily lends itself to interest rate targeting, the first transmission mechanism subsequently is referred to as the Keynesian transmission mechanism.

The immediate target in this transmission mechanism is the short-term nominal interest rate (i_{st}). In the United States, this short-term rate is the federal funds rate. In other countries, it is a comparable overnight rate. According to the theory, open market purchases increase the supply of loanable funds and push i_{st} downward. Open market sales have the opposite effect.

Changes in the immediate target, in turn, affect the *long-term real* rate of interest (r_{lt}) in the same direction. The real interest rate is the intermediate target because the objective is to affect real spending (y). If rational economic agents think in real terms, and not nominal terms, it is the real rate that the central bank must change.

Not only is the intermediate target a real interest rate, but it is also a long-term rate. The objective is to affect spending on (business and consumer) durable goods, which are the most cyclically volatile component of real aggregate spending (y). If the objective of monetary policy is to tame the business cycle, it must have an impact on expenditures for these types of goods. The relevant rate of interest for durable goods expenditures, of course, is the long-term rate.

According to Model I, then, open market purchases lower the short-term nominal interest rate which, in turn, reduces the long-term real interest rate. A lower long-term real interest rate encourages spending on durable goods. Higher capital goods expenditures increase the level of real GDP. Open market sales have the opposite impact. Tighter monetary policy increases nominal and real rates and reduces real aggregate expenditures for durable goods.

Model II of the transmission mechanism uses monetary aggregates as targets. The immediate target is the quantity of base money; the intermediate target, the money supply. It is called the classical transmission mechanism because it focuses on the relationship between quantity of money and aggregate spending. This money-spending nexus has long been the center of attention for economists in the classical quantity-theory tradition.

In the case of Model II, open market purchases increase the quantity of bank reserves and the monetary base. An increase in base money leads to an increase in the money supply as banks use the newly created reserves to extend their lending activity. Increases in the money supply, in turn, result in higher nominal spending. That is, nominal GDP increases. Open market sales initiate the opposite sequence that ultimately leads to a decline in nominal GDP.

Two features of this transmission mechanism deserve notice. First, the linkages in this transmission mechanism are concepts encountered before. The linkage between quantity of base money (the immediate target) and the money supply (the intermediate target) is the base money multiplier. The velocity of circulation of money, of course, links the quantity of money (the intermediate target) and the level of nominal GDP (policy objective).

Second, while the changes in open market operations ultimately affect nominal GDP, it is the impact on the composition of GDP that is of greatest interest. Although many (in the quantity theory tradition) acknowledge that changes in money affect real GDP in the short-run, it is long-term consequences of changes in money that most concerns them. Maintaining long-run price stability and, thus, the integrity of money is the primary goal of monetary policy.

Choice of Monetary Targets

A target employed in the conduct of discretionary monetary policy generally must satisfy the following two criteria. First, the target must be a variable that the central bank can control. Second, the target must be linked in a predictable way to the ultimate objective or objectives of policy.

The second criterion ultimately rests with correctness of the theory underlying the transmission mechanism. The importance of correctly specified linkages becomes apparent when considering the implications for targets that are not selected. Selection of an interest rate target, for example, implies the rejection of monetary aggregates as targets. In this case, the growth rate of the money supply becomes a residual. Money is permitted to grow at whatever rate is necessary in order to maintain the interest rate target. Such neglect of money growth worries economists in the quantity theory tradition because it may lead to greater inflation.

Alternatively, targeting a monetary aggregate (such as base money) means that interest rates are free to fluctuate. This is an issue for proponents of Model I. From their perspective, greater variability in interest rates is likely to result in larger fluctuations in expenditures for durable goods and less macroeconomic stability.

The decision by the Federal Reserve in the United States to use interest rate targets reflects the Fed's judgment that interest rate targets better satisfy the two criteria stated above than do monetary aggregates. A critique of that judgment is presented in Chapter 6.

Interest Rate Targeting in the U.S.

Countries using interest rate targeting generally employ an overnight loan rate as the target. In the United States, that rate is the federal funds rate. The federal funds rate is the interest rate charged on loans of immediately available funds. Such funds are also known as same-day funds because borrowers have access to the funds on the day of the loan. This is necessary for federal funds transactions because most are one-day loans.

A sizable portion of the activity in the federal funds market involves the lending of bank reserves owned by commercial banks and held at Federal Reserve Banks. Such loans involve the transfer of ownership of these reserve balances from one bank to another. Repatriation of these balances occurs when the loan is repaid.

The Federal Reserve System in the United States has used the federal funds rate as a target for decades. Only for a brief interlude (1979–1983) did the Fed switch to targeting monetary aggregates. Since that time it has continuously targeted the federal funds rate.

When the Federal Reserve uses this target, it does not actually set the federal funds rate. Commercial banks are free to negotiate loans of federal funds at any mutually agreeable interest rate. As an illustration of how

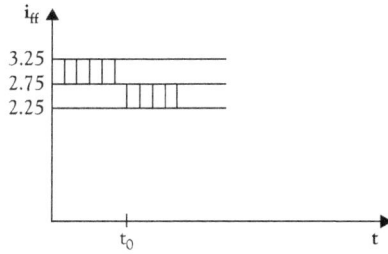

Figure 5.2 Federal funds market

federal funds rate targeting works, consider Figure 5.2 above. Each plot shows the daily trading range for the federal funds rate.

The initial target is 3%. In maintaining that target, the Federal Reserve permits the federal funds rate to fluctuate between 2.75% and 3.25%. Its task is to provide reserves to the banking system in quantities that will cause banks to price federal funds loans in the 2.75% to 3.25% range. If, for example, there is excess demand for federal funds when the rate is 3.25%, the Federal Reserve must make up this deficiency by providing more reserves to the federal funds market. It does so through open market purchases of U.S. Treasury securities. By accommodating the excess demand for federal funds, the freely negotiated federal funds rate does not rise above 3.25%.

On the other hand, if there is an excess supply of federal funds at the 2.75% federal funds rate, the Federal Reserve must intervene to keep the rate from falling below 2.75%. To decrease the quantity of reserves in the market, the Federal Reserve must undertake open market sales of Treasury securities. The media often describes this activity as: "The Fed drained reserves from the banking system."

A change in Federal Reserve policy is brought about by changing the level of the federal funds rate target. A higher target signifies tighter monetary policy; a lower target, monetary ease. Assume, in this example, that the central bank lowers the target from 3% to 2.5%. This occurs at time t_0 in Figure 5.2. The Fed must now provide a volume of reserves that keeps the federal funds rate between 2.25% and 2.75%. It accomplishes this through more liberal provision of reserves to the federal funds market, i.e., through increased open market purchases.

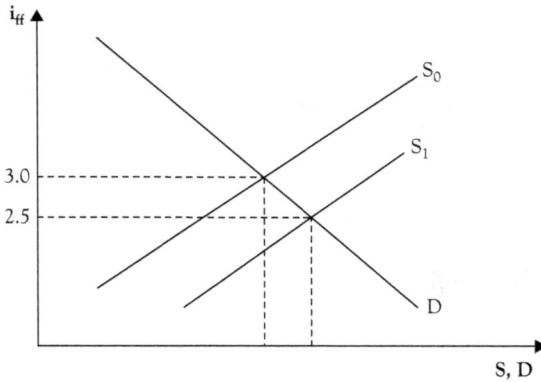

Figure 5.3 *Federal funds market*

A graphical version of this policy change appears in Figure 5.3, where the federal funds rate is plotted against the quantity of federal funds supplied and demanded. The initial federal funds target was 3%. The lower federal funds rate target of 2.5% is achieved through an increase in the supply of federal funds. The supply curve shifts from S_0 to S_1 as a consequence of open market purchases by the Federal Reserve.

Two caveats related to interest rate targeting are mentioned here. First, the supply of money becomes a residual in the monetary process. The growth rate of money is whatever rate is necessary to maintain the interest rate target. As noted earlier, this approach has the potential for kindling or accelerating inflation.

Second, the ability of a central bank to successfully implement interest rate targeting is affected by the state of inflationary expectations. This was a problem for the Federal Reserve in the 1970s. In Figure 5.2, excess demand for federal funds at the rate of 3.25% caused the Fed to increase the supply of reserves through open market purchases. If this increase in bank reserves (and the accompanying increase in money growth) occasions an upward revision of inflationary expectations, the result is an even greater demand for bank reserves. Excess demand pressures reappear. To keep the rate from rising above 3.25%, the Federal Reserve must again provide additional reserves to the banking system. The growth rate of the money supply again increases, and impacts further on inflationary expectations.

In this scenario, interest rate targeting gives rise to dynamic instability in credit markets. It is driven by inflationary psychology, but fueled by central bank money creation. Once inflationary psychology becomes entrenched, an increase in the interest rate target may not signify monetary restraint. It may be a manifestation of prior monetary ease.

The Federal Reserve and the Great Recession of 2008–2009

The United States experienced the sharpest recession since the Great Depression in 2008–2009. It quickly became known as the Great Recession. The Federal Reserve reacted strongly and even introduced monetary measures that were unprecedented.

Initially, the Federal Reserve employed conventional policies. Through open market purchases, it lowered the targeted federal funds rate. From a level of 4.25% in December, 2007, the target was lowered in a series of steps to near zero by the end of 2008 (0–0.25%).

The seriousness of the downturn became more apparent when uncertainties about the financial viability of banks came into question. Banks became more reluctant to lend to businesses as well as to each other. Activity in credit markets, and especially the commercial paper market and the federal funds market, declined dramatically. Many businesses experienced considerable difficulty in arranging for short-term financing.

Sensing the potential for financial panic, the Federal Reserve assumed the role of lender of last resort. It informed banks, and also participants in financial markets in general, that the Fed was ready to supply the necessary liquidity through the discount window. In order to encourage more borrowing, the Fed increased the volume of reserves auctioned through its Term Auction Facility (TAF). This auction process allowed banks to competitively bid for reserve funds at the discount window. This contrasted with the normal pricing procedure where discount rate is set by the Fed.

The Federal Reserve broadened the scope of its lending activity beyond its lending to depository institutions. It opened credit facilities and provided funds to a number of new markets. Among those impacted were the commercial paper market, money market mutual funds, investment banking firms, and security dealer firms. In an effort to further stabilize the financial system, the Fed made a multi-billion dollar loan to an insurance company (AIG) teetering on the verge of bankruptcy.

There were also two major asset-purchase programs undertaken by the Fed. Referred to as quantitative easing (QE1 and QE2), they departed from the Fed's historical pattern of purchasing short-term U.S. Treasury securities through its open market operations. Both resulted in a massive infusion of reserves into the banking system. The magnitude of these purchases was reflected in the Fed's balance sheet, which grew by approximately 150%.

QE1 primarily involved the purchase of large quantities of mortgage securities, many directly from commercial banks. Because payment for the securities was in bank reserves, these Fed purchases improved the liquidity of banks. It also improved the quality of the bank asset holdings by replacing lower quality loans with cash. With fewer nonperforming loans on their balance sheets, bank capital adequacy ratios were favorably impacted.

The purchase of mortgage securities introduced a new asset into the Federal Reserve balance sheet. It also marked a movement away from its historical pattern of providing credit to markets in a more neutral manner, and toward the selective provision of credit. Individual banks selling mortgage instruments to the Fed were favored, as was the mortgage market more generally. This movement to selective credit controls was discussed in Chapter 4 (pp. 88–91).

Because of its enormous impact on monetary aggregates, the QE1 program shares some characteristics with the classical transmission mechanism which targets monetary aggregates (Model II above). However, there are significant differences, as is evident in Exhibit 5.2. The QE1 instrument variable was the purchase of mortgage instruments rather than U.S. government securities. Moreover, while the monetary base moved sharply higher under QE1; that was not the immediate target. The immediate objectives were to stabilize the banking system and to support the housing market. The ultimate policy objective was an increase in aggregate spending, but linkages specifying how that occurs were not clearly indicated. Thus, there is some ambiguity about the transmission mechanism for QE1, as indicated by the question mark for the intermediate target.

Model	Instrument variable	Immediate target	Intermediate target	Policy objective
QE1	MTG →→	Stabilize banks & housing Mkt.	→→ ? →→→	P·y (P or y)
QE2	OMO →→→	i$_{LT}$ →	r$_{LT}$ →→→	P·y (P or y)

Exhibit 5.2 QE1 and QE2 Transmission Mechanisms

QE2 involved the Federal Reserve purchase of $600 billion of long-term U.S. Treasury securities. The immediate target was to reduce the long-term nominal interest rate (Exhibit 5.2). Although not often noted by the Fed, rational economic agents think in real terms and the intermediate target was a lower long-term real interest rate. The ultimate policy objective was to increase aggregate spending, specifically spending on durable goods which are typically financed with long-term credit.

It is noteworthy that transmission mechanism for QE2 differed from the transmission mechanism for interest-rate targeting, or Model I (pp. 111–112). The immediate target for QE2 was a long-term nominal rate; for Model I, it was the short-term nominal rate. The intermediate target and the policy objective were the same.

The QE2 transmission mechanism had an historical antecedent in the early 1960s. At that time, it was referred to as operation twist. The magnitude of U.S. Treasury security purchases was much more modest in the 1960s, but the motive in both cases was to alter the shape of the yield curve by lowering the long-term interest rate.

CHAPTER 6

Critiques of Monetary Policy

Critiques of Monetary Policy

Fiat money is a relatively new phenomenon. It has been in use slightly more than three-quarters of one century. Thus, how historians will eventually evaluate this experiment with fiat money is yet to be determined. It is probably an understatement to suggest that the U.S. experience with this type of money, to this point, has not been an unmitigated success. Because fiat monies are controlled by governments, what historians must eventually assess is how governments have performed.

Monetary policy is reasonably transparent and the performance of governments as custodians of fiat money has not gone unnoticed. The critiques discussed in the next sections are not concerned with situations where seigniorage is the principal motive of monetary authorities. Rather, the focus is on the practice of discretionary monetary policy in countries where macroeconomic management is the driving force behind policy.

A common thread in critiques of monetary policy is the critical role that knowledge plays in the successful implementation of discretionary monetary policy. The critiques that follow demonstrate the multi-dimensional nature of the knowledge issue.

One very important kind of knowledge required of central bankers is knowledge about the performance of the economy, something that is necessary if monetary authorities are to know whether monetary ease or tighter money is the appropriate policy. When knowledge does exist, it is not always apparent that central bankers will be in a position to utilize that knowledge. Political considerations may interfere. Central banks are also expected to understand how the policy they enact is transmitted to the economy, and how those affected will respond to that policy. Finally, it is important for central banks to know what effect, if any, the infusion of new money has on relative prices and the allocation of resources across markets.

Friedman: Rules vs. Discretion

Milton Friedman argues that the use of discretionary monetary policy has resulted in increased economic instability. The problem is not with the use of fiat money. Rather, it is with the procedures employed by central banks to implement monetary policy, specifically the use of discretionary policy. Replacing that type of policy with a monetary rule would greatly reduce economic uncertainty, especially uncertainty about the future course of monetary policy. This would provide a much better climate for productive activity and eliminate much of the economic instability occasioned by the use of fiat money.

In fashioning this position, Friedman's posture is diametrically opposed to those who favor the use of discretionary policy. Proponents of discretionary policy maintain that its use can greatly improve macroeconomic performance. Appropriate application of policy instruments will both reduce short-run business cycle fluctuations and bring us greater long-run price stability. Monetary stimulation during a recession, for example, will shorten the recession. If too much inflation is the problem, tighter monetary policy is in order.

Friedman's case against discretionary policy is that those implementing such policies most often do the wrong thing. Two principal reasons for this are: 1) politics, and 2) ignorance. By doing the wrong thing, those implementing discretionary policies make economic conditions worse rather than better.

Politics

Economic analysis of monetary policy often proceeds as if this policy were conducted in a political vacuum. That decidedly is not the case. Monetary policy is carried out by government, and the political consequences of a policy action receive careful consideration. What is considered rational policy from a political perspective can differ significantly from that implied by economic theory. If political considerations dominate, those implementing discretionary policy may, with good reason, deliberately select the incorrect economic policy.

Political considerations can affect monetary policy even in countries (such as the United States) that have a fairly independent central bank. When, for example, is a good time for the central bank to invoke a tighter monetary policy that results in higher nominal interest rates? From a political perspective, the likely answer is never. As a consequence, central bankers bold enough to undertake such policies can expect politicians to sharply criticize their actions. That may be enough for policymakers contemplating such action to reconsider.

Elections cycles also create problems for those implementing discretionary monetary policy. In the absence of political pressure, introducing a policy change too close to an election can be interpreted as politically motivated. For central bankers in democratic countries who are sensitive to such charges, this might inhibit the implementation of an otherwise appropriate change in monetary policy.

A second way that election cycles influence monetary policy is through the actions of politicians concerned about an imminent election. They might exert pressure on central bankers to undertake policies favorable to their election (or reelection). Research suggests that, in the United States, this may be the rule rather than the exception. For the period from 1951 to the end of the 1970s, Robert Weintraub found that changes in Presidential administrations generally resulted in changes in monetary policy in a direction consistent with the economic views of the President.[1] Given that Ronald Regan ran on a platform of reducing inflation, Paul Volker's disinflationary policies in the 1980s are an indication that Weintraub's results extend beyond his sample period.

A prototypical case study in central bank accommodation was President Richard Nixon's reelection campaign in 1972. Inflation was increasing at the time, and economic theory implied a tighter monetary policy. Tighter money, however, was not the policy of choice for President Nixon. From his perspective, such policies had cost him the Presidential election in 1960. He was not interested in a repeat of that experience. Federal Reserve Chairman Arthur Burns accommodated President Nixon's desire that monetary policy not be tightened. Nixon won the election, but at a considerable cost to the economy.

Ignorance

A second reason for the failure of discretionary policies is ignorance. The existence of time lags presents a major problem for those attempting to implement discretionary policies. These lags imply that policy carried out today has its impact in the future. Selection of the appropriate policy, then, requires the ability to forecast accurately. Economists, however, are notoriously weak when it comes to forecasting future economic activity. This ignorance is especially pronounced for turning points in the economy, where one would anticipate significant changes in discretionary policy.

Three time lags encountered when implementing discretionary policy are the recognition lag, the execution lag, and the impact lag. To illustrate the difficulties introduced by these time lags, refer to Figure 6.1. Real GDP (y) is plotted against time (t). The business cycle peak occurs at time t_1, with GDP equal to y_1.

The decline in economic activity commencing at time t_1 is not discovered until time t_2. One reason for this lag is that published economic data generally are a record of the past, and turning points in economic activity often are not discovered in these data until well after they happen. For this cycle, the time interval $(t_2 - t_1)$ is the recognition lag. It is the time that elapses between when the economy changes, and when policy makers know about the change.

The policy response is not instantaneous. In the case of monetary policy, the central bank must both adopt a new policy and implement that policy. These events too, require time. Assume that the policy response, which is additional monetary stimulation, occurs at time t_3. The time interval $(t_3 - t_2)$, then, is the execution lag. This is the amount time that elapses between recognition of the problem and when policy makers undertake appropriate policy action.

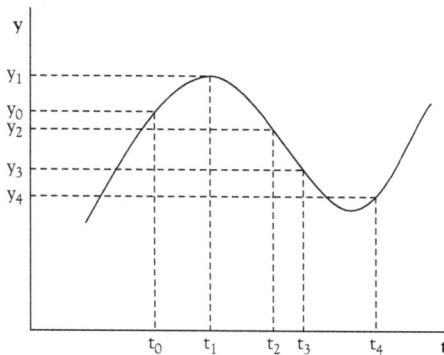

Figure 6.1 Discretionay policy with time lags

The impact of this policy action, likewise, is not instantaneous. Rather than occurring at a point in time, it is distributed over a period of time. The precise timing of the impact is unknown. Friedman's estimates for the U.S. economy are that it will have little (or no) impact for the first 9–12 months, with the total impact occurring over a period of years.

Simplifying, assume that the impact of monetary policy does occur at a single point in time (t_4). By that time, the economy has already entered the expansionary phase of the business cycle. To moderate business cycle fluctuations, this phase of the cycle calls for monetary restraint. Instead of monetary restraint, however, the central bank is providing monetary stimulus. It has done the wrong thing. Monetary policy will accentuate the business cycle upswing and, in doing so, it increases the amplitude of the business cycle.

Given the existence of these time lags, appropriate discretionary policy for this economic cycle requires that the central bank undertake simulative policy before the business cycle downturn occurs, e.g., at time t_0. The wisdom to do so, however, requires that (central bank) economists correctly forecast the impending peak at t_1. Their inability to accurately forecast turning points, or ignorance, generally precludes that.

Friedman's x-Percent Money Growth Rule

Even though it is inadvertent, central bank implementation of discretionary monetary policy often makes things worse rather than better. For that reason, Friedman recommends scrapping discretionary policy. In its place, the central bank should follow a rule and increase the money supply at a constant rate. If, for example, a rate of 4% is selected, the central bank increases the money supply 4% each year. That is Friedman's x-percent money growth rule.

The particular growth rate that is selected is less important than selecting one. A rate in the neighborhood of 4% may be desirable, however, because it approximates the secular growth rate for production. Synchronizing the growth of money and output would permit (proximate) long-run price stability.

Friedman maintains that the potential benefits of employing a monetary growth rule are enormous. The principal one is a more stable economy. A volatile monetary policy contributes to economic instability, thus increasing the amplitude of the business cycle. Use of a monetary rule effectively eliminates this source of cyclical instability.

A second benefit is increased long-run economic growth. As monetary policy becomes more predictable, the uncertainty faced by those in private business is greatly diminished. This lowers the risk premium in interest rates, and will increase the rate of capital formation in the economy. More capital formation leads to increased worker productivity and higher living standards.

Finally, use of a monetary rule will eliminate of secular inflation. Had the Federal Reserve employed such a rule in the past half-century, the great depreciation that occurred in the purchasing power of the U.S. dollar would have been avoided. Elimination of secular inflation will enhance the services provided by money, especially those eroded by unremitting inflation.

Despite these potential benefits, Friedman is aware of the forces militating against adoption of a monetary rule. A major force is the spiritual legacy of the Enlightenment. The great scientific and economic achievements of the past several centuries have nurtured the sense that man has the ability to make things better through manipulation and control. When placed in a monetary context, this perspective makes it easier for central bankers to inspire confidence in their ability to successfully manage monetary affairs.

Public confidence in central bank stewardship is reinforced by central bank resistance to a monetary rule. Given the complexities of a modern economy, central bankers are often given much greater credit for their ability to manipulate aggregate economic activity than is warranted by experience. The general public often basks in the comfort of a central bank that is "in control." As human beings, it is natural that central bankers find such deference to their skills and influence quite flattering. It is contrary to human nature to expect them to embrace the prospect of replacing their reasoned judgments with a mechanical procedure that greatly diminishes their social significance.

The Road Not Taken: A Friedman Case Study

It is not possible to know what would have happened had the Federal Reserve followed Friedman's x-percent money growth rule. That is a road

Table 6.1 Dynamic Equation of Exchange for the U.S. Economy
(Average Annual Growth Rate: 1959–2012)

	dM/M	+	dV/V	=	dP/P	+	dy/y
Actual U.S. data	6.9		−0.2		3.6		3.1
Data with x-percent money growth	4.0		−0.2		−0.3		4.1

Source: Actual U.S. Data: Federal Reserve Bank of St. Louis data base (FRED)

not taken. It is possible, however, to *simulate* what Friedman had in mind through the prism of the dynamic version of the equation of exchange. In Table 6.1, that relationship is utilized to compare actual data for the 53-year period from 1959–2012 with hypothesized data using Friedman's x-percent growth rule.

From 1959–2012, annual U.S. money growth (dM_2/M_2) averaged 6.9%. Long-run velocity was relatively stable, declining at an average annual rate of 0.2%. Real Gross Domestic Product growth (dy/y) averaged 3.1%. With too much money chasing too few goods, the United States experienced an average secular inflation rate (dP/P) of 3.6% per year.

By comparison, assume the Federal Reserve implements Friedman's x-percent growth rule by increasing the money supply by 4% each year. The velocity of money is relatively stable with the assumed annual growth rate (dV/V) the same as the actual growth rate for 1959–2012: −0.2%. Friedman argued that such monetary stability would lead to higher economic growth. Accordingly, the average annual growth rate for real GDP is 4.1%. That was the actual rate of growth for the 1950s, the decade prior to the implementation of Keynesian economic policies during the J.F. Kennedy administration.

For the period under consideration, Friedman's x-percent money growth rule yielded long-run price stability. Prices, on average, declined 0.3% per year. Such price stability is comparable to that experienced by the United States when the country was using fiduciary money (prior to 1933).

Had the United States actually experienced such price stability, the considerable erosion in the services provided by money would probably not have occurred. For example, with long-run price stability, money would have continued to serve as a viable store of value. In addition, Friedman would likely make the case that United States would have been spared the dislocations and economic hardships associated with the

Great Inflation of the 1970s and the ensuing disinflation of the 1980s. He also might argue that, with the x-percent money growth rule, the United States would not have suffered through the Great Recession of 2008–2009. A policy of providing new money at a steady rate (instead of pushing short-term interest rates close to zero for an extended period) would reduce the likelihood of an asset bubble in housing that was at the epicenter of the Great Recession.

Interest Rate Targeting

Central banks in relatively advanced countries generally employ interest rate targeting to implement discretionary monetary policy. Excluding the four-year interlude from 1979–1983, the Federal Reserve System in the United States has targeted interest rates for several decades. While the analysis that follows applies to interest rate targeting more generally, the issue is framed within the context of U.S. monetary policy.

Federal Reserve interest rate targeting conforms to the transmission mechanism described as Model I in the previous chapter. The instrument variable is open market operations (OMO). The immediate target is the short-term interest rate (i_{st}). The rate selected for this purpose is the federal funds rate, or the rate on immediately available funds. While it is a nominal interest rate, the intermediate target is the long-term *real* interest rate (r_{lt}). The ultimate policy objectives are the price level and aggregate spending.

The Fed encounters two very difficult problems when attempting to implement policy through this transmission mechanism. First, it is using a nominal interest rate target in a world where rational economic agents think in real terms. The interest rate of importance, then, is the unobservable real interest rate. Second, the transmission of monetary policy occurs across the term structure of interest rates. The immediate target is a short-term interest rate, but the critical variable is the long-term rate of interest.

The Nominal/Real Dichotomy

The success of Federal Reserve monetary policy is contingent upon control of the real interest rate. Rational economic agents on both sides of the credit market think in real terms and, if one is to change their behavior through policy, it is the real interest rate that counts. Unlike the nominal interest rate, however, the real interest rate is unobservable. The difficulty presented here is that one cannot readily control something that does not lend itself to measurement. That problem is compounded when precision is required. That is generally the case, however, because policymakers employing nominal immediate targets most often change those interest rate targets in increments of one-quarter to one-half percent.

Control of the unobservable real rate of interest is hypothesized to occur via changes in the Federal Reserve's nominal interest rate target (the federal funds rate). As noted in Chapter 3, however, the nominal rate of interest, too, is comprised of nonobservable components: inflationary expectations; default, money, and income risk premiums; and, time preferences. Each of these components reflects the subjective valuations of millions of market participants. Because subjective valuations of individual economic agents are prone to change, one must operate on the premise that they do. That is, inflationary expectations, risk premiums, and time preferences are incessantly changing.

If these nonobservable components of the nominal rate of interest are unstable, when the Fed changes its nominal interest rate target, it cannot know whether the real interest rate is increasing, falling, or staying the same. If a policy-induced higher real interest rate indicates a tighter monetary policy, and a policy-induced lower real rate the opposite, the Federal Reserve does not know whether its monetary policy is tighter, easier, or neutral.

To illustrate, three different scenarios are presented in Table 6.2. They are designated as Cases I, II, and III. The first scenario (Case I) is the initial condition. The nominal interest rate is 5%, which is also the Fed's targeted interest rate. With a 2% expected rate of inflation, the real interest

Table 6.2 The Nominal Interest Rate and Its Components

	i	r	(dp/p)*	Risk premium	Marginal rate of time preference
Case I	5	3	2	½	2½
Case II	6	4	2	½	3½
Case III	4	2	2	½	1½

rate is 3%. The latter is apportioned into a risk premium and a marginal rate of time preference.[2]

Assume, initially, that the Federal Reserve attempts to tighten monetary policy. In Case II, it raises its target for the nominal interest rate to 6%, and provides reserves less liberally to the banking system. With tighter credit conditions, the nominal rate increases to the desired level. Assuming no change in inflationary expectations, the real rate increases to 4%. The higher real rate of interest leads to reduced capital goods expenditures, and a higher marginal rate of time preference. In this scenario, the Fed thinks that monetary policy is tighter and, indeed, it is. This is how monetary policy with interest rate targeting is supposed to work.

With the subjective preferences of economic agents constantly changing, however, the world is much more complex than this. For example, do these Case II numbers still constitute tighter monetary policy if the higher real interest rate would have occurred as a result of market activity alone? Commence again with Case I initial conditions, i.e., i = 5% and r = 3%. Now, assume an increasingly robust economy with businessmen becoming more optimistic. Their increased time preferences for current expenditures are expressed in the form of a greater demand for capital goods. Tighter credit conditions lead to a higher nominal rate (6%) and a higher real rate (4%). Case II numbers again prevail.

Superimpose upon these events an increase in the Federal Reserve's target for the nominal interest rate—from 5% to 6%. The Fed's objective is to increase the real interest rate by 1% (from 3% to 4%). In this case, the Fed does not need to adjust how it is providing reserves to the banking system. The higher interest rates come about through market activity alone, and do not reflect any change in Fed policy. When the Federal Reserve adjusts its interest-rate target upward, that target is simply following the market rate.

This is a case where the Federal Reserve thinks monetary policy is tighter when, in fact, it is not. Errors of this kind are likely when the real interest rate follows a pro-cyclical pattern. If business managers and consumers become more optimistic during a business cycle expansion, their greater optimism is expressed in the form of an increase in their time preferences for current expenditures. The real (and nominal) interest rate rises. If the Federal Reserve simultaneously becomes concerned about the exuberant economy, it will move to tighten monetary policy. As in the example above, however, it will erroneously interpret the market-driven rise in interest rates as policy-induced.

The Federal Reserve is prone to making the opposite kind of error when the economy is contracting. Business managers and consumers become more pessimistic. They experience decreases in their time preferences for current expenditures, and the real (and nominal) interest rate falls. The Fed, in an attempt to stimulate aggregate demand, lowers its interest rate target. With the nominal and real rate already falling, the Fed is unable to distinguish market-induced declines in rates from those occasioned by Fed policy.

This scenario is captured in Case III (Table 6.2). Commencing with the initial condition (Case I), declines in the real and nominal rate occur in response to reduced time preferences. The nominal rate falls from 5% to 4%; the real rate, from 3% to 2%. Simultaneously, the Federal Reserve lowers its target for the nominal interest rate from 5% to 4%. Its intent is to lower the real rate by a similar amount (from 3% to 2%). The Federal Reserve does not need to adjust its provision of reserves to the banking system, because both the nominal and real rates reach their targeted levels through market activity. This is a case where the Fed thinks that monetary policy is easier when, in fact, it is not.

Thus, there are serious reservations concerning the Federal Reserve's ability to effectively control the real rate of interest. When the Fed changes its nominal interest rate target, it does not know with any assurance either the magnitude or direction of policy-induced changes in the real rate of interest.

The Term Structure Problem

A second problem the Federal Reserve confronts when targeting interest rates relates to the term structure of interest rates. Not only does the Fed not know whether adjustments in its immediate target result in the desired change in the real interest rate, but those policy changes also must be transmitted across the term structure of interest rates. The Federal Reserve's operating target is the short-term nominal rate, but its intermediate target is the *long-term* real interest rate.[3]

The rationale for this transmission mechanism (Model I) is discussed in Chapter 5. Outlays for durable goods, both business and consumer, are more easily deferred than are expenditures for nondurable goods. As a consequence, durable goods account for much of the volatility in aggregate spending. Attempts by policy makers to influence aggregate spending (and the price level), then, are geared towards controlling expenditures for those types of goods. With durable goods purchases frequently financed through the issue of long-term bonds, those purchasing durable goods are sensitive to the long-term rate of interest. It follows that, when the Fed employs interest rate targeting, it must target the long-rate.

Precisely how the Federal Reserve successfully navigates the term structure and, simultaneously engineers changes in the real interest rate, is not clear. Moreover, various theories of the term structure (discussed in Chapter 3) do not provide much help. If anything, they cast additional aspersion upon the Fed's ability to successfully implement discretionary policy through interest-rate targeting.

Explanations based on the segmented markets hypothesis, for example, are not encouraging. If market participants adhere strongly to their maturity preferences, there is little likelihood that policy-induced changes in the short-term interest rate target will be transmitted across the term structure to long-term rates of interest. Federal Reserve control, in turn, is marginalized.

On the other hand, information requirements implied under the unbiased expectations and the liquidity preference theories present an even more serious obstacle for those conducting monetary policy. First, the Fed must have prior knowledge of the term structure of inflation premiums and the term structure of risk premiums. Second, it must know how those term structures are changing independent of monetary policy. Finally, it must also know how a given change in its short-term interest rate target will affect both of those underlying term structures. Compounding the Fed's information problem is the fact that both inflationary expectations and risk premiums are imbedded in the term structure of interest rates, and not directly observable.

It is clear that the U.S. central bank faces serious information problems when attempting to target long-term real interest rates through use of a short-term nominal operating target. If the Federal Reserve acts as if it can orchestrate desired changes in aggregate spending and the price level through this procedure, it is committing what Friedrich von Hayek called "the pretense of knowledge."[4] It is pretending to know things that, in fact, it does not.

A Recent U.S. Case Study

This knowledge problem confronting the Federal Reserve is a good illustration of what happens when the criteria for selecting monetary targets (discussed in the previous chapter) are not satisfied. Because it is not possible to accurately measure the long-term real interest rate, the Federal Reserve is employing a target it cannot control. Moreover, lack of knowledge of the long-term real rate also means the linkages in Model I are not predictable.

U.S. monetary policy from 2004–2006 exemplifies the difficulties encountered when these monetary target criteria are not met. Starting in June, 2004, the Federal Reserve increased its target for the federal funds rate fifteen consecutive times. As a consequence, the federal funds rate target in April, 2006 was 4.75% versus 1.00% in the first half of 2004. Those changes are chronicled in Table 6.3.

Many observers routinely describe these upward adjustments in the federal funds rate target as tighter monetary policy. There are serious doubts, however, about such an interpretation. It is true that other short-term nominal rates increased along with the federal funds rate. The three-month Treasury-bill rate, for example, rose from 1.17% to 4.60% between June 1, 2004 and March 1, 2006.[5]

But, as previously noted, higher short-term nominal interest rates do not necessarily mean tighter monetary policy. Long-term nominal interest rates actually fell during the same 21-month period. The rate for 20-year U.S. Treasury securities declined from 5.45% to 4.74%. These changes in both long-term and short-term rates for U.S. Treasury securities are reflected in Figure 6.2. It depicts the shapes of the term structure of interest rates for U.S. Treasury securities on both June 1, 2004 and March 1, 2006. The yield curve in 2006 became noticeably flatter.

Lower long-term nominal interest rates, however, are not the issue. It is long-term real interest rates, and not nominal rates, that are critical for

Table 6.3 Federal Funds Rate Target

Date	Level (percent)
2006	
March 28	4.75
January 31	4.50
2005	
December 13	4.25
November 01	4.00
September 20	3.75
August 09	3.50
June 30	3.25
May 03	3.00
March 22	2.75
February 02	2.50
2004	
December 14	2.25
November 10	2.00
September 21	1.75
August 10	1.50
June 30	1.25
2003	
June 25	1.00

Source: Board of Governors of the Federal Reserve System

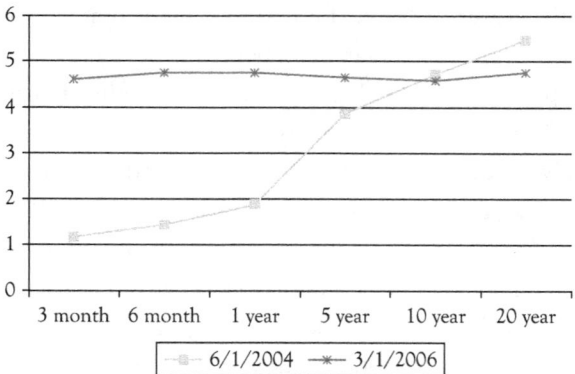

Figure 6.2 Term structure of interest rates US treasury securities: Constant maturity

Source: Board of Governors of the Federal Reserve

economic decisionmakers. If monetary policy was, indeed, tighter during this 21-month period, long-term real interest rates must have increased while nominal rates were falling. Moreover, the increase in real rates must have occurred as a result of monetary policy and not due to other factors such as an increase in default risk or changes in time preferences for current expenditure. While such a scenario appears doubtful, no one knows for certain. Hence, the appropriate answer to the question about whether monetary policy is tighter is: "I don't know."

Monetary Aggregates and Monetary Control

Recent Issues with Monetary Control

After facing difficulties with interest-rate targeting during and after the Great Recession (2008–2009), the Federal Reserve embarked on several massive asset purchase programs described as quantitative easing. Those carried out during the Great Recession are discussed in Chapter 5 (pp. 118–119).

While the Fed's asset purchase programs were not advanced with the stated intent of increasing monetary aggregates, they did. In doing so, these programs raised an additional issue relating to central bank control of the money supply. These issues are discussed in the context of the general money supply model in Chapter 4 (equation 4.2).

The magnitude of the Federal Reserve's asset purchases caused the monetary base in the United States to explode. Base money increased more than threefold from 2007 and 2012, and was largely in the form of increases in bank reserves. Under more normal circumstances, one would anticipate a massive increase in the money supply, huge increases in spending, and the potential for the largest inflation in U.S. history.

To date, none of these things have happened. The reason is that banks have not used this infusion of bank reserves to extend additional bank credit (and expand deposit money). Instead, those reserves were almost entirely held in the form of excess reserves.

In the money supply model, an increase in the aggregate bank excess reserve ratio causes the money multiplier to decrease. In this case, because the increase in bank excess reserves was so massive, the multiplier collapsed.

As shown in equation 6.1, the large increase in the monetary base was virtually entirely offset by a fall in the money multiplier. In the context of these changes the consequences for money (which did rise) were minimal.

$$M = B \; m. \tag{6.1}$$
$$\leftarrow \quad \uparrow \quad \downarrow$$

This experience has important implications for monetary policy. It differs from the liquidity trap explanation advanced by early Keynesians. In that case, the central bank increases the money supply and it has no effect on spending. People hold rather than spend the additional money, and velocity falls. When this happens, monetary policy is ineffective.

In the present case, the effectiveness of monetary policy is questioned for a different reason. Unlike the previous case, the money supply does not increase, or it does so minimally. What distinguishes the recent experience is collapse of the money multiplier as shown in 6.1.

The precipitous fall in the multiplier represents a breakdown in a transmission mechanism for monetary policy. In Chapter 5, the transmission mechanism employing monetary aggregates as targets was Model II. In that transmission mechanism, what links base money to the money supply is the base money multiplier. The usefulness of that transmission mechanism is predicated upon a predictable relationship for transforming base money into money. It is that relationship that fell apart.

This experience raises serious questions concerning the ability of the Federal Reserve to control the money supply. When combined with the lackluster results from interest rate targeting, it appears that both transmission mechanisms I and II for implementing discretionary monetary policy did not perform as expected during and after the Great Recession (2008–2009).

Why the Federal Reserve Needs an Exit Strategy

The massive infusion of bank reserves (and base money) into the U.S. financial system from 2008 to the present leaves the Federal Reserve with an important legacy issue. If the United States is to avoid significant future inflation, the Fed must undertake future monetary policy that (largely) removes that base money from the system or, alternatively, provides banks with an incentive to not activate the massive excess reserves they now hold. The description of how the Federal Reserve plans to do this is known as the Fed's exit strategy.

The magnitude of the problem confronting the Federal Reserve is apparent in Table 6.4. From 2007–2012, bank reserves and base money increased by 1,611% and 213%, respectively. These dramatic increases were not reflected in the money supply (M_2) which rose by only 37.7%. This surprisingly modest number is the result of the collapse of the base money multiplier (m), which fell by 57.5%. These data comport with the directional changes in equation 6.1 above.

The problem confronting the Federal Reserve is about what happens in the next business cycle expansion. Since the most recent business cycle trough (June, 2009), businesses and households have behaved very cautiously. Credit demands by both sectors have been restrained, and economic growth has been tepid.

Table 6.4 Bank Reserves, Base Money, Money Supply, and the Money Multiplier for the United States 1999–2012

Year	Reserves	Base money	M2	m
1999	88.7	574.2	4525.8	7.88
2000	84.5	607.1	4801.6	7.91
2001	85.9	641.2	5222	8.41
2002	88.1	697.1	5595.6	8.03
2003	93.3	740.9	5986.8	8.08
2004	96.1	776.8	6269.2	8.07
2005	96.6	806.6	6269.2	8.07
2006	94.9	835	6865	8.22
2007	94.2	850.5	7264.8	8.54
2008	232.4	1010.2	7764.5	7.69
2009	944.4	1796.6	8385.5	4.67
2010	1143.7	2031.7	8593.1	4.23
2011	1576.5	2539	9221.5	3.63
2012	1611.9	2662	10006.4	3.79

Source: Monetary Trends, (various issues, Federal Reserve Bank of St. Louis)

If, in the future, both businesses and households throw caution to the wind, and become very aggressive in their demands for credit, banks (which are awash in liquidity) are in a position to accommodate them. Moreover, banking competition makes them inclined to do so. If an individual bank refuses a customer's demand for credit, that customer is likely to take his/her banking business to another bank.

Meeting these credit demands means an increase in money growth, which has the potential to accelerate sharply. The acceleration in money growth, in this case, is occasioned by an increase in the base money multiplier. As banks reduce their holdings of excess reserves, the aggregate excess-reserve ratio falls and the money multiplier rises.

The potential impact on the money supply is captured by assuming that the multiplier returns to its prerecession level of 8.54 (2007). If that adjustment had occurred in 2012, the impact on the money supply for that year is shown in 6.2.

$$M2 = \$22,733.5 = B_{2012} * m_{2007} = \$2,662.0 * 8.54 \qquad (6.2)$$

With a multiplier of 8.54 in 2012 (and assuming the same 2012 level for base money), the money supply would have been \$22,733.5 billion for that year instead of the recorded level of \$10,006.4 billion. That represents a 127.2% increase in the money supply. In other words, the money supply has the potential to grow this much if the multiplier were to return to its prerecession level. If all of this money growth were to occur in a single year, the average price would increase by a magnitude of the same order.[6] Thus, the potential exists for much higher inflation than occurred in earlier episodes such as the Great Inflation of the 1970s. That is why the Federal Reserve needs an exit strategy.

Rational Expectations

Economists know that a person's expectations affect the economic decisions made by that individual. Rational expectations theory is concerned with how those expectations are formed and, also, how economists model those expectations. Much of this theory was developed in response to the use of large macroeconometric models (by business and government). Statistical in form, these models were an adjunct to the Keynesian revolution in macroeconomic theory. The models often contained several hundred equations, and were used for forecasting purposes. Keynesian economists used the models to advise governments about the consequences of different activist policies, while those in the private sector used them as an aid in business decision-making.

Many of the equations in macroeconometric models were behavioral in nature. That necessitated the modeling of expectations, even though those expectations were unobservable. Proxies for these unknown expectations were most often obtained by assuming that economic agents have adaptive expectations. With this approach, the expected value of a variable was estimated as a weighted sum of past values of that same variable. Historical time series data were employed for rendering concrete estimates.

Econometric models constructed using this methodology often result in large forecasting errors, and economists in the rational expectations tradition have a ready explanation for this. Reliance on adaptive expectations as a proxy for actual expectations is an inherent weakness of the models. For, modeling human behavior in this way is tantamount to assuming that economic agents are irrational. The reason is that economic agents with adaptive expectations make systematic errors. That is, they repeatedly make the same mistakes.

An alternative to assuming that expectations are adaptive is to assume they are rational. Rational individuals are not restricted to using past information (such as past values of variables) when forming their expectations. Their expectations are formed by taking into account all information that is worthwhile acquiring. Agents behaving in this fashion are said to have rational expectations. Once the models of economists incorporate rational expectations, economic agents are less prone to making the same mistakes repeatedly—systematic errors. Moreover, such rational behavior has implications for the effectiveness of economic policy.

If economic policy affects economic agents in a significant way, then it is rational for them to take the effects of that policy into account. Furthermore, if those administering policy behave consistently, economic agents will learn how that policy is implemented under different economic

Table 6.5 Policy Impotence Theorem

Period	M	V	=	P	y
I	→	↑		→	↑
II	↑	↓		→	→

circumstances. Once they do, individuals will adjust their behavior to the policy, and make necessary behavioral changes *before* any change in policy is undertaken. Because adjustment to the policy has already taken place, no behavioral response follows any predictable change in economic policy. In rational expectations theory, this result is known as the Policy Impotence Theorem.

When behavior is rational in this sense, discretionary policy loses its effectiveness. An example of such policy impotence in the context of rational economic behavior is chronicled in Table 6.5. In Period I, individuals anticipate monetary ease that will occur in Period II. Sensing that they will be able to finance additional expenditures at a lower rate in the near future, they adjust their current expenditures upward. Producers respond by increasing production in Period I and, in the absence of a change in the money supply, the offsetting entry in the equation of exchange is an increase in the velocity of circulation of money (V↑).

In period II, the central bank increases the money supply to stimulate aggregate demand. However, there is no increase in spending because rational economic agents anticipated this monetary stimulation and have already adjusted their spending plans (in Period I). In Table 6.5, the money supply increases in Period II but GDP expenditures remain the same. The offsetting entry is a decline in velocity (V↓). The monetary ease engineered by the central bank in Period II has no effect on current spending, i.e., it was impotent.

The rational expectations argument against the use of discretionary policy does differ from that of Friedman (and the monetarists) in one important respect. In Friedman's case, discretionary policy does not work because policymakers are either ignorant or subject to political influence. For the rational expectations economists, discretionary policy does not work because those affected by the policy are the opposite of ignorant. They are too smart (or rational).

The Austrian Perspective on Monetary Policy

Economists in the Austrian tradition generally favor "hard money." They find it vexing that a monetary economist such as Milton Friedman favors reliance upon markets everywhere except in his area of expertise, the realm of money. The Austrian position is that money is too important to be left to government. Instead, money and all monetary relations should be determined through exchange activities in the marketplace. Because fiduciary money was a spontaneous market development, and fiat money was not, Austrians generally favor reestablishing fiduciary money by returning to the gold standard.

If the quantity of money and all monetary relations are determined by market participants, government has no monetary role. There is no monetary policy. For that reason, Austrians are against all monetary policy as practiced under fiat money regimes. That would include Friedman's monetary growth rule as well as all variations of discretionary policy.

At the center of the Austrian critique of monetary policy is the concept of the price level. The importance attached to the idea of an average price dates back to the early 20th century, when Irving Fisher argued that the value of money should be standardized.[7] By this, he meant that the objective of government monetary policy should be to stabilize the average price, or the price level. While Fisher was unsuccessful in his crusade to standardize money, the concept of the price level subsequently assumed a life of its own. After governments mandated the use of fiat money, the price level became a variable subject to manipulation by monetary authorities.

Despite the efforts by central banks to manage the price level, Austrians give the concept little credence. For them, the price level has no significance independent of its component parts—the individual prices. To the extent that there is an average price, it is an aggregation of these individual prices. In a market setting, each individual price has meaning, or informational content. Each is an expression of the subjective valuation that individuals have placed on that object. Viewed collectively, a set of individual prices represents relative valuations.

With no rigid dichotomy separating microeconomics and macroeconomics, the significance Austrians attach to individual prices is not restricted to the realm of microeconomics. They are equally important in a macroeconomic setting. Hence, when central banks manipulate the price level, without regard to its constituent parts, they destroy the informational content of individual prices. In doing so, they disrupt the critical role that prices play in coordinating the diverse economic activities that collectively make up the aggregate economy.

Assume, for example, that a central bank employs monetary policy to stabilize the average price. The problem here is that market participants may have preferences that are not consistent with an unchanged exchange value for money. In the absence of monetary policy, they may have valued money either more highly or less highly than before. If they valued money more highly, their preferences were consistent with deflation rather than price stability. Alternatively, placing a lower value on money would result in inflation.

When money is a strictly a market phenomenon, inflation, deflation, and price stability are all possible outcomes. Moreover, there is no analytical basis for favoring one of these outcomes over the others. This view is antithetical to conventional thinking, especially with regard to deflation. Most contemporary policymakers, and many economists, consider deflation highly undesirable—something that must be avoided at all costs.

The source of this bias against deflation is the Great Depression experience, when deflation was accompanied by an unprecedented drop in production. To generalize from this episode, however, is ahistorical. Data generally do not affirm such a linkage between deflation and economic decline.[8] Moreover, given our experiences with fiat money, it seems much more likely that massive economic decline would be accompanied by significant inflation rather than deflation.

In contrast to the conventional view, Austrians do not readily dismiss deflation when it is the natural outcome of economic activity. Deflation generally occurs when a country's growth rate for production exceeds the growth rate of money. Money becomes more scarce in relation to goods, and that tends to occasion an increase money's exchange value. This happened in the United States during the last third of the 19th century. The country was on the gold standard, and there were few new discoveries of gold to augment the world's gold supply.

Data for this period, assembled by Christina D. Romer, appear in Table 6.6. Deflation averaged 1.36% per year from 1869 to 1899. In contrast

Table 6.6 Prices and Production in the United States: 1869–1899 (percent change)

Year	Real GNP	GNP-Implicit price deflator
1869–1879	5.38	−3.23
1879–1889	3.21	0.03
1889–1899	3.82	−0.85
1869–1899	4.13	−1.36

Source: Romer (1989), pp. 1–37.

to the conventional view of deflation, this period of falling prices was not one of economic calamity, or even malaise. Instead, it was a period characterized by much innovation and very rapid industrialization. The average growth rate for production was considerably higher than average growth during the 20th century. Moreover, production growth was, by far, most rapid in the decade with the highest rate of deflation (1869–1879).

Historical episodes like this suggest that changes in the general price level (such as inflation or deflation) generally do not cause problems when they are driven by market forces. A collateral issue, though, is whether problems arise when the source of the price-level change is monetary manipulation by the central bank, and not market adjustments occurring in response to changing market conditions.

Austrians answer this question in the affirmative. Consider, initially, what happens when changes in the quantity of money are a derivative of the market process. Allocation of additional resources to the production of new money, in this case, originates with decisions made by individual market participants. As a response to market demand, the additional money was, in a sense, "ordered" by those market participants. It reflects their preferences concerning the use of scarce resources. Any change in prices brought about by the new money is, likewise, a part of the same market process whereby individual plans and preferences are rendered consistent with one another.

The situation is entirely different when the source of a change in money is the central bank. In this case, the additional money is not ordered by market participants. As a consequence, it is not a part of the market adjustment process that renders individual plans consistent with one another. Instead, the new money is a disruptive force in markets. By changing relative prices, compared to what they otherwise would have been, it destroys the informational content of market prices. Relative prices no longer represent that delicate balance necessary to coordinate economic activity across markets.

A critical price often distorted by monetary policy is the real interest rate. This rate reflects the time preferences of market participants. A given real rate specifies how much future consumption economic agents are willing to sacrifice in order to have more present consumption. By affecting how consumers distribute consumption across time, the real interest rate plays an essential role in the intertemporal allocation of resources.

When monetary policy brings about a change in the real interest rate, it adversely affects the intertemporal allocation of resources. It does so by distorting the informational content present in a market-determined real rate of interest rate. The new real interest rate occasioned by monetary policy emits the "wrong" signal to market participants, and the economic coordination brought about by market prices is disrupted. Production plans of firms are no longer consistent with the preferences of their customers.

The disruptive influence of monetary policy is illustrated by comparing situations with and without monetary policy. The market under scrutiny is the loanable funds market. Prior to the introduction of monetary policy, the real interest rate plays its allocative role. In doing so, it renders the plans of all economic agents consistent with one another. Those plans are reflected in the demand and supply curves D and S in Figure 6.3.

Plan consistency occurs at the market clearing rate r_0. The quantity of loanable funds supplied, S_0, shows abstinence from present consumption by economic agents. It is exactly equal to the quantity of loanable funds demanded, D_0. This demand originates with consumers desirous of consuming more than their incomes, and producers borrowing to acquire capital goods.

Intertemporal economic coordination occurs in this case because the real interest rate is transmitting the correct information to market participants. The amount of resources released from (net) present consumption is precisely absorbed by those borrowing to purchase capital goods. Those abstaining from present consumption are choosing an increased amount of future consumption. That demand for future

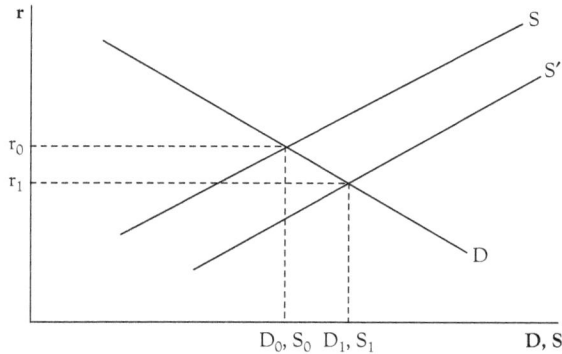

Figure 6.3 Market for loanable funds

consumer goods will be accommodated by a larger volume of future output made possible by current capital formation.

Such intertemporal coordination of economic activity no longer prevails once monetary policy is introduced. The reason is that the information contained in the real interest rate is distorted by monetary policy. To show this, assume the central bank increases the money supply. The supply curve for loanable funds shifts to the right (to S′). There is now an excess supply of loanable funds at r_0, and the real interest rate falls to r_1.

While this lower real interest rate does clear the credit market, the rate did not fall due to any change in the plans of individual economic agents. It did not fall, for example, because consumers desire to defer more consumption to the future, or because producers choose to purchase fewer capital goods. A lower real interest in either of those circumstances would convey such a change in preferences to others in the market.

Instead, the source of the decline in the real interest rate is the additional funds made available through monetary policy. By falling without any changes in the plans of economic agents, the informational content of the real interest rate is compromised. At r_1, the real interest rate is below the level (r_0) that renders the diverse plans of economic agents consistent with one another. The new real interest rate is transmitting the wrong signals to market participants.

Producers are encouraged to purchase more capital goods, and they bid the necessary resources away from those producing consumer goods. The problem is that this redirection of resources is not consistent with consumer preferences. Consumers have not chosen to tradeoff additional present consumption for more future consumption. This miscommunication brought about by monetary policy has important macroeconomic consequences. At some point, this misallocation of resources will have to be rectified. The endplay involves economic recession with all of its attributes—falling (and possibly negative) profits, idle capital goods, unemployment, and business bankruptcies.

From the Austrian perspective, then, all monetary policy is disruptive rather than beneficial. It destroys the informational content of market prices. Unfortunately, to undo the pernicious effects of such policy is not a costless proposition. Requisite adjustments in the allocation of resources are similar to those that are necessary at the end of a protracted war. Large quantities of resources are misallocated in the sense that they are used to produce war materials that are no longer useful. These situations often lead to a period of falling output and increased unemployment.

Case Study: Federal Reserve Policy and Malinvestment

Austrian economists make the case that recent Federal Reserve policy is instructive for understanding the nature of boom/bust cycles. First and foremost, such cycles are generated by central banking policy. In that context, the Great Recession of 2008–2009 is viewed as a prototypical business depression emanating from prior interest rate policies of a central bank, in this case the Federal Reserve.

In the first decade of this century, Federal Reserve policymakers were convinced that the U.S. economy was facing the specter of deflation. As noted earlier, such a prospect is generally viewed by those implementing monetary policy as an anathema. The Federal Reserve reacted accordingly.

The antidote for deflation was an increase in aggregate spending. From the Federal Reserve's perspective, lower interest rates were in order. That they engineered. The target rate for the federal funds rate was reduced sharply, and eventually held at 2.0% or less for more than three years—from November, 2001 to December, 2004. The intent was to defuse deflationary forces by encouraging greater spending on durable goods.

The problem, from an Austrian perspective, is that interest rates are something more than prices subject to manipulation by the Fed. They are critical for the intertemporal coordination of economic activity. By manipulating interest rates, the Federal Reserve destroyed the informational content of market prices and disrupted the allocation of resources across time.

The policy-induced lower interest rates encouraged more roundabout productive activities, i.e., a greater production of durable goods. That, indeed, was the Fed's intent. The difficulty is that consumers did not, through their market activity, initiate the order for these additional capital goods. They came about because consumers were reacting to a false set of prices engineered by the central bank.

In this episode, a sizable portion of the addition to the country's capital stock was in the form of new housing. The housing boom contributed, temporarily, to a more robust level of economic activity. That boost in activity was not to be permanent. From the Austrian perspective, the bloated housing stock was a manifestation of a previous misallocation of resources—one induced by Federal Reserve policy. It is what Austrians refer to as malinvestment. The market correction, or the bust, played out as the Great Recession of 2008–2009.

Postscript

These critiques provide insight into the kinds of problems confronting modern governments as they manage fiat money systems. Collectively, they explain why those charged with that responsibility often perform poorly and sometimes fail. Their task is a daunting one. As an indication, critics cite the following skills and/or conditions as those most likely to result in a favorable discretionary monetary policy experience.

- Monetary policy is driven by economic considerations, and is generally unaffected by politics.
- While individuals in the private sector are unable to accurately forecast the future (and especially business cycle turning points), individuals employed by the central bank are able to do so.

- The unobservable long-term real interest rate is amenable to control by the central bank.
- The money supply is amenable to control by the central bank.
- Even though economic agents in the private sector are affected in a dramatic way by monetary policy, they make no attempt to anticipate and respond to future central banking policy.
- The role that prices, and especially the interest rate, play in the coordination of economic activity can be safely disregarded by monetary authorities.

Notes

Chapter 1

1. For an extended version of this discussion of monetary systems, see Gerdes (1997).

2. It is erroneous to assert, as some economists do, that fiat money has no intrinsic value. From this perspective, the marginal subjective value of fiat money, when used for nonmonetary purposes, is zero. We know that is not the case. Examples of possible value generating nonmonetary uses for fiat money are using stacks of fiat money as doorstops, paperweights, or as kindling in the fireplace.

3. Had consumers preferred fiat money, issuers of fiduciary money would have voluntarily accommodated those preferences.

4. Some make the case that the U.S. government did not leave the gold standard until August 15, 1971. On that date, President Richard Nixon closed the U.S. gold window to all foreign central banks. From 1933 to 1971, gold had a very limited monetary role. Governments allowed central banks to settle imbalances of payments through gold shipments. It is difficult, however, to make the case that the United States was on the gold standard from 1933 to 1971 when it was illegal for all households and private businesses in the United States to possess any monetary gold.

5. Deflation is also self-limiting with fiduciary money. Market forces tend to increase the quantity of commodity money. If a government reduces the quantity of fiduciary money to offset this, the ratio of fiduciary money to commodity falls. The lower limit for this ratio is zero. When the ratio approaches zero, the government is no longer able to offset the rising production of commodity money. Increases in the total quantity of money eventually bring to an end the deflation.

6. Traveler's checks are demand deposits owned by bank customers but drawn on a commercial bank. Historically, they were used for making payment outside a country. Because individuals are now able to access funds in their checking accounts through ATM machines located in foreign countries, aggregate traveler's checks have fallen to less than 1% of M1. Thus, these deposits are frequently disregarded in discussions of M1.

Chapter 2

1. The source for Fisher's analysis is: Fisher, Irving, *The Purchasing Power of Money* [Fairfield, NJ: Augustus M. Kelley, 1913 (Reprinted 1985)].
2. Refer to Pigou (1917) for his version of the quantity theory of money.
3. One important distinction is that the Cambridge demand for money is a static concept. It typically applies to a given point in time. By contrast, Fisher's velocity of circulation of money happens over a period of time.
4. Keynes (1936), p. 207.
5. Friedman and Schwartz (1963).
6. In an attempt to simplify Fisher's macroeconomic analysis, some state that he assumed that velocity and real output are held constant. That is incorrect. For a discussion of this mischaracterization of Fisher's analysis, see Gerdes (1986), pp. 66–72.

Chapter 3

1. An economic unit is a decision-making entity. These units are generally classified as a household, business, or governmental unit.
2. This method for classifying participation was employed by Van Horne (1998). It was also used in early flow-of-funds studies. See Goldsmith (1965).
3. Böhm-Bawerk (1959). This translation and compilation is from Böhm-Bawerk's books on capital and interest written from 1884–1914. Chapter I in Book IV of Volume II is entitled "Present and Future in Economic Life."
4. Böhm-Bawerk referred to this as contract or loan interest.
5. This analysis abstracts from other factors that might make for a positive price of credit even if individuals are indifferent between goods now and goods in the future. They would include transactions costs and risk. The issue of risk is discussed in some detail below.
6. von Mises (1949). A well-known student of von Mises, Murray Rothbard, defined interest in the same way. See Rothbard (1962).
7. Transactions costs, which are not discussed here, are also neglected. They, too, can affect the level of the real interest rate.
8. No risk premium is necessary if investors are generally risk-neutral or risk-preferred.
9. Yield curves with other shapes are also possible. Generally, they are a combination of those depicted in panels (a), (b), and (c). One such possibility is the humped yield curve. It initially rises, reaches a peak, and subsequently descends.

10. The following discussion of theories of the term structure draw from Van Horne (1998).

11. Irving Fisher is credited with an early version of this theory. See Fisher (1896), pp. 23–29 and pp. 91–92.

12. J. R. Hicks developed the liquidity preference argument. See Hicks (1946), pp. 145–147.

13. Modigliano and Sutch (1966), 178–97.

Chapter 4

1. The profit on this loan is not 5% because interest on this deposit is not the only cost to the bank. Additional costs are in the form of resources banks employ in servicing customer loan and deposit accounts.

2. Derivation of this equation appears in Appendix A at the end of this chapter.

3. The derivation of the M1-multiplier is found in Appendix B at the end of the chapter.

4. Until recently, banks in the United States earned no income on bank reserves. In 2008, the Federal Reserve began paying interest on reserves held at Federal Reserve Banks (MBD). The current annual rate for these deposits is 0.25%.

5. For a summary of these changes in discount rate policy, see Stevens (2003).

6. It is possible for Bank A to acquire additional reserves from other banks. In that case, Bank A will not have to contract its loan portfolio. However, the total quantity of reserves in the banking system has not changed. With a higher reserve requirement, this means that other banks in the system must contract their loan portfolios.

7. For a discussion of sweeps and their implications, see Anderson and Rasche (2001), pp. 51–72.

8. Exclusion from reserve requirements was an important feature of MMDA deposits, which were created in the Garn-St. Germain Act of 1982. However, there was an important qualification attached to this exclusion. No more than six withdrawals were allowed per month. If this qualification was not met, an MMDA deposit was treated as a transactions account (subject to reserve requirements applicable to those accounts).

9. The absence of an adequate financial infrastructure may result from the fact that these countries are poor. It may not. These countries may be poor because of a weak market structure. Their governments, in many cases, have actively discouraged the development of markets. It should come as no surprise that these countries cannot rely upon markets for the implementation of monetary policy.

Chapter 5

1. Banks, businesses, and individuals had three weeks to turn in their gold to the government. There were limited exceptions. Individuals could keep $100 in gold coins; coin collectors were allowed two specimens for any issue. So much gold was confiscated, that the U.S. government deemed it necessary to construct a large vault at Fort Knox, Kentucky. For a discussion of the U.S. nationalization of gold, refer to Weatherford (1997), chapter 12.
2. Had consumers preferred fiat money, issuers would have provided it volitionally. As noted, absence of the convertibility option makes life easier for issuers of money.
3. Fischer (1996). England left the gold standard in 1931, and 20th century fiat money inflation is dated from that year.
4. This seigniorage curve is discussed in McCulloch (1982). He refers to it as a monetary Laffer curve, and notes that it was introduced by Martin Bailey long before the concept was employed by Arthur Laffer. See Bailey (1956).
5. To simplify the analysis, other influences on money demand (such as interest rates and income) are assumed to be fixed.
6. Other types of economic policy are available for use by governments. They include fiscal policy, exchange-rate policy, and wage and price controls. The focus here is on monetary policy.

Chapter 6

1. Weintraub (1978), pp. 341–362.
2. This is the rate of time preference for lenders. For a discussion, refer to Chapter 3, pp. 39–41.
3. In the early 1960s, and again in the recession of 2008–2009, the Federal Reserve introduced a program that employed the long-term nominal interest rate as the operating target. This procedure was dubbed operation twist because it attempted to twist the yield curve by lowering long-term interest rates. When the operating target is the long-term rate, the transmission mechanism does not navigate the yield curve. The current discussion of interest rate targeting abstracts from these special cases.
4. von Hayek (1989), pp. 3–7.
5. Interest rates are for constant maturities. *Source*: Board of Governors of the Federal Reserve System.
6. It is unlikely that all of the money growth would occur in a single year. Annual inflation rates, then, would depend on the number of years it takes for the money expansion to occur. Those rates are also affected by production growth and changes in money demand.

7. In the spirit of the Enlightenment, Fisher maintained that "our unstable and unstandardized monetary units are among the last remnants of barbarism and are out of place in present-day civilization." See Fisher (1919), pp. 156–157.

8. See Atkeson and Kehoe (2004), pp. 99–103. Using data for 17 countries and covering more than 100 years, they find virtually no link between deflation and depression.

References

Anderson, G. R., & Rasche H. R. (2001, January–February). Retail sweep programs and bank reserves, 1994–1999 *review* (pp. 51–72). Federal Reserve Bank of St. Louis.

Atkeson, A., & Kehoe J. P. (2004, May). Deflation and depression: Is there an empirical link? *American Economic Review: Papers and Proceedings, 94*, 99–103.

Bailey, M. (1956, April). The welfare cost of inflationary finance. *Journal of Political Economy.*

Böhm-Bawerk, E. (1959). *Capital and interest* (Vol. I–III). South Holland, IL: Libertarian Press.

Cagan, P. (1956). The monetary dynamics of hyperinflation. In M. Friedman (Ed.) *Studies in the quantity theory of money.* Chicago: University of Chicago.

David P. A., & Solar, P. (1977). A bicentenary contribution to the history of the cost of living in America. *Research in Economic History 2*, 1–80. (Reprinted in McCusker, J. J. (2001). *How much is that in real money?: A historical commodity price index for use as a deflator of money values in the economy of the United States.* Worcester, MA: American Antiquarian Society.)

Fischer, H. David (1996). *The great wave: price revolutions and the rhythm of history.* New York, NY: Oxford University Press.

Fisher, I. (1913). *The purchasing power of money.* Fairfield, NJ: Augustus M. Kelly. (Reprinted 1985).

Fisher, I. (1930). *The theory of interest.* New York, NY: Augustus M. Kelly. (Reprinted 1961).

Fisher, I. (1896, August). Appreciation and interest. *Publications of the American Economic Association XI.* 23-29 & 91-92.

Fisher, I. (1919, March). Stabilizing the dollar. *American Economic Review, 9*, 156–157.

Freidman, M., & Schwartz, A. (1963). *A monetary history of the United States.* Princeton, NJ: Princeton University Press.

Gerdes, W. D. (1997). A taxonomy of monies from the consumer's perspective. *The Journal of Economics 23*(3), 21–29.

Gerdes, W. D. (1986, Spring). Mr. Fisher and the classics. *The American Economist*, 66–72.

Goldsmith, R. (1965). *The flow of capital funds in the postwar economy.* New York, NY: National Bureau of Economic Research.

Hicks, J. R. (1946). *Value and capital* (2nd Ed.). London, UK: Oxford University Press.

Keynes, J. M. (1936). *The general theory of employment, interest, and money.* New York, NY: Harcourt, Brace & World.

McCulloch J. H. (1982). *Money and inflation: A monetarist approach* (2nd ed.). New York: Academic Press.

Modigliano, F., & Richard Sutch. (1966, May). Innovations in interest rate policy. *American Economic Review, 56*, 178–97.

Phelps, B. E. H., & Hopkins, S. V. (1956, November) Seven centuries of the prices of consumables, compared with builders' wage-rates. *Economica, 296–314*.

Pigou, A. C. (1917, November). The value of money. *The Quarterly Journal of Economics 32*, 38–63.

Romer, C. D. (1989, February). The prewar cycle reconsidered: New estimates of gross national product: 1869–1908. *Journal of Political Economy*, 1–37.

Rothbard, M. (1962). *Man, economy and state: A treatise on economic principles* (Vol. 1). Princeton, NJ: D. Van Nostrand.

Stevens, E. (2003, May). The new discount widow. *Economic Commentary*, Federal Reserve Bank of Cleveland.

U.S. Bureau of Labor Statistics. *Consumer price index*. Retrieved from: http://www.bls.gov/cpi

Van Horne, J. C. (1998). *Financial market rates and flows* (5th ed.). Englewood Cliffs, NJ: Prentice-Hall.

von Hayek, F. (1989, December). The pretence of knowledge. *American Economic Review, 79*, 3–7.

von Mises, L. (1949). *Human action: A treatise on economics* (3rd rev. ed.). San Francisco, CA: Fox and Wilkes (Reprinted 1966).

Weatherford, J. (1997). *The history of money*. New York, NY: Three Rivers Press.

Weintraub, R. E. (1978, April). Congressional supervision of monetary policy. *Journal of Monetary Economics, 4*, 341–362.

Index

Index

OTHER TITLES IN ECONOMICS COLLECTION

Philip Romero, The University of Oregon and Jeffrey Edwards,
North Carolina A&T State University, Editors

- *Managerial Economics: Concepts and Principles* by Donald Stengel
- *Your Macroeconomic Edge: Investing Strategies for the Post-Recession World* by Philip Romero
- *Working with Economic Indicators: Interpretation and Sources* by Donald Stengel
- *Innovative Pricing Strategies to Increase Profits* by Daniel Marburger
- *Regression for Economics* by Shahdad Naghshpour
- *Statistics for Economics:* Shahdad Naghshpour
- *How Strong Is Your Firm's Competitive Advantage?* By Daniel Marburger, Daniel
- *A Primer on Microeconomics:* Thomas Beveridge
- *Game Theory: Anticipating Reactions for Winning Actions:* Mark L. Burkey
- *A Primer on Macroeconomics:* Thomas Beveridge
- *Economic Decision Making Using Cost Data: A Guide for Managers* by Daniel M. Marburger
- *The Fundamentals of Money and Financial Systems* by Shahdad Naghshpour
- *International Economics: Understanding the Forces of Globalization for Managers* by Paul Torelli
- *The Economics of Crime* by Zagros Madjd-Sadjadi
- *Money and Banking: An Intermediate Market-Based Approach* by William D. Gerdes

Announcing the Business Expert Press Digital Library

Concise E-books Business Students Need
for Classroom and Research

This book can also be purchased in an e-book collection by your library as
- a one-time purchase,
- that is owned forever,
- allows for simultaneous readers,
- has no restrictions on printing, and
- can be downloaded as PDFs from within the library community.

Our digital library collections are a great solution to beat the rising cost of textbooks. e-books can be loaded into their course management systems or onto student's e-book readers.

The **Business Expert Press** digital libraries are very affordable, with no obligation to buy in future years. For more information, please visit **www.businessexpertpress.com/librarians**. To set up a trial in the United States, please contact **Adam Chesler** at *adam.chesler@ businessexpertpress.com* for all other regions, contact **Nicole Lee** at *nicole.lee@igroupnet.com*.

www.ingramcontent.com/pod-product-compliance
Lightning Source LLC
Chambersburg PA
CBHW050113210326
41519CB00015BA/3944